'Never mind, Maggie,' my father used to say to Mother, 'I'll take you away when the yellow's on the broom.'

My family were travelling people. Others describe travellers as 'mist-folk' – or 'tinkers', a name we hate.

Most of the year we lived in tents but we spent the winter months in an old house. Mother called it 'a dark wee hole' and we waited impatiently for the spring and our escape into the open air again . . .

THE YELLOW ON THE BROOM

the early days of a traveller woman

Betsy Whyte

WARNER BOOKS

Obviously this story contains words which are traveller cant
or of Scottish origin. Their meaning will usually be apparent,
but these words are fully explained on pages 179 to 186.

Warner Books
A Division of
Little, Brown and Company (UK)
Brettenham House
Lancaster Place
London WC2E 7EN

To Mother and Father
and Linda

'What's that you're doing, lassie?'

My mother's voice startled me as I was sitting in the tent combing my hair—when I should have been away to work. The others had left over half an hour earlier.

Then I heard Mary's voice answer Mother. 'I'm just washing out some clothes.' 'I can see that you're washing but, lassie dear, you can't hang your knickers out like that there with all the men passing by looking at them. Look, lassie, double them over like this or pin that apron over them and they will dry just as quickly. If Johnnie comes home and sees your knickers hanging there, he will be your death.'

Mother came back into the tent muttering to herself 'God knows what he was doing marrying a scaldie for anyway. You can put sense into them no way.' Then she spoke to me. 'Are you not going to any work today?' 'I'm just going, Ma.'

When I stepped out of the tent, I met Mary. She had not argued back with Mother but had done as Mother told her. 'Are you going to the field?' she asked. 'Aye,' I answered. 'Are you?'

As the two of us made our way down the old road she asked me 'Did you hear your mother at me again this morning?' 'Mother is only telling you for your own good. Remember the beating you got from Johnnie when you sat in front of the men with your legs apart?' (Traveller men hate their wives doing things like that. A traveller woman would never do so, anyway.)

Mary was not a traveller. Johnnie, my mother's nephew, had met her when he was working in Perth. She had worked in Stanley Mill and went into Perth some weekends, for her mother lived there. She had been cooped in the mill for five years and the fresh air and outside life since she married Johnnie had agreed with her. But she was a bit befuddled with some of our strange customs.

'Ach, you'll soon learn,' I told her. 'You've only been married four months.' We were all really fond of Mary.

Soon we reached the field where several men and women were pulling turnips. My father, uncles and their wives, Johnnie (Mary's man) and also a man called Hendry Reid who none of us was very fond of. Hendry was too soulless-hearted, having been known to kick and batter his wife and children—and horse when he had one.

This Hendry Reid was talking away as they worked. 'That man is always ganshin',' I said to Mary. 'Some of the men are sure to lose the head with him one of these days. He is always bragging about how he can get other men's wives, and about what he done in the War, but my mother says that he hid himself in a cave in Argyllshire all the time of the War. His poor mother was trauchled to death carrying food for miles to him. Oh aye, he was a brave soldier!'

We picked up our hukes (sickles, if you like) and started to pull the neeps. Mary was not very good at it, but Johnnie helped her to keep up. Soon it was after midday and, although it was October, the sun was beaking down on us. Hendry was still ganshin'. My father and the other men and women could have seen him in hell. Nothing could have been more nerve-racking than his loud, squeaky, incessant voice.

2

Then Dad shouted to Mary and me. 'You two lassies go down to that farm and see if you can get a drop of milk, and if you see the old keeper ask him for a seed of tobacco for me. I'll have the water boiling for you coming back, so hurry up! Johnnie, you go for sticks—and Liza, you can look for some clean water.' (Liza was Mother's brother's wife.)

It was more than a mile to the farm, so Mary and I walked quickly down the old road. 'I could do with a smoke,' Mary said. 'Aye, and me too,' I answered.

Then Mary looked startled. 'Look over in that field. What are all they men doing over there?' 'That's shooters,' I told her. 'Do you not see their guns? They are just stopped for a smoke.' 'Smoke!' I said again. 'What's about asking them for tobacco?' 'I'm game if you are,' Mary said. So we climbed through the paling and walked across the field. 'They can only say aye or no,' I told Mary.

There must have been about twenty men with plus-fours, deerstalker hats and leather boots. As we drew near they stared at us. 'What are you doing here, and what do you want?' a huge man with a red mouser, and a face to match, shouted. He was holding a whisky flask in his hand, as were several of the others.

'I wonder if any of you would have a wee bit tobacco to spare?' I asked. 'It's for my father.' I thought Beetroot Face was going to have a fit. 'Get out of here before I put the dogs on you!' The other men were all laughing. But one of them said 'Wait a minute. Give this to your father' and he threw a tin which landed at my feet. 'Just take the tin with you,' he said. I lifted it and took to my heels, Mary after me. We threw ourselves over the fence and collapsed, breathless and giggling, at the side of the old road.

'He is a civil man, that one with the face like a harvest moon,' I said. 'You wouldn't want for your supper if everybody was like him.' Mary looked blankly at me and said 'Eh?' I sometimes forgot that she wasn't a traveller, and didn't understand this travellers' habit of saying the opposite of what they meant.

'Never mind,' I said to her, opening the tin of tobacco. 'This is not tobacco, it's shag,' I said. 'Let me see.' Mary took the tin. 'It *is* tobacco. The very best of tobacco.' 'Well, I've never seen tobacco like that,' I answered her, 'but I'm going to make a fag with some of it anyway. Do you have a match?' 'No,' she said. 'Then we are as well worried as hung. We have tobacco now and no match. We'll get one down at the farm.'

'But wheesht, Mary! I hear something coming up the road. Come through the paling into the field and let it pass. It's a car of some kind.' It was a shooting brake. 'Sit down Mary, and they won't see us. Some of they gentry,' I said, as it passed along the narrow road. 'Come on and we'll hurry to the farm for milk.'

The back door of the farm was wide open and the

savour of cooking and baking nearly took the heart from me. I hadn't as yet broken my fast. The farm-wife was a pleasant person. When we told her our errand she said 'Aye, plenty, lassies—but it's been skimmed. Give me your flagon and I'll fill it for you.'

'Did you come down the way?' she asked, as she ladled the milk into the can. 'Aye,' I answered. 'Then you must have seen the Duchess passing, in a shooting brake, and her two bonny wee lassies with her. The Duke is up there somewhere with the shooters. They say he is a good shot. He's the Duke of York, you know, and he's married to Elizabeth, one of the Bowes-Lyons from Glamis Castle. His father is the King,' she went on.

'Do you mean that one of they men shooting up the road is the King's son?' I asked. 'That's what I'm telling you,' she answered. Mary and I exchanged glances. 'Shaness, shaness,' I whispered. The farm-wife was very pleased and excited at having seen the gentry. 'The Duchess is likely away up with their lunch,' she said. 'My two laddies are away beating for them.'

'Would you like a piece?' she asked. She came out with two large pieces of still-warm scone. 'Oh! Thank you very much, Missis.' Mary rived into her piece but me, being a traveller, thought about my daddy pulling heavy swedes and without even a smoke. The scone would have choked me if I had eaten it past him. 'If you don't mind, Missis, I'll take my piece up to my father. He is working just up the road a bit.' 'Och, just you eat it up, lass. I have plenty and I'll give you some to take away with you.' I sank my teeth into the scone. It was dripping with syrup and never, I thought, had I tasted anything better. 'Well, goodbye Missis, and thank you kindly for being so nice to us. God bless you.' 'Away you go, lassies, it's nothing.'

'I'm not going up the road,' I said to Mary. 'Come on and we'll cut across the fields.' As we hurried over the fields Mary said 'You forgot to ask for a match.' 'Oh, so I did,' I answered. 'I'm that worried about begging that tobacco. Don't tell my daddy, mind.'

As we approached, Father asked sarcastically 'Where did you go for the milk, to Kirriemuir? I'm sure I could have been in Inverness the time you've taken.'

Instead of answering him I took the tin of tobacco out of my pocket, opened it and held it out to him. 'Where did you get that, lassie?' 'Lying on the ground,' I said truthfully. 'Look, boys!' Daddy turned to let them all see it.

Oh, barry! They were so pleased. Few of them had seen tobacco like this before. 'That's the kind of tobacco the gentry smoke,' Father explained to them. 'One of them must have lost it. Maybe one of those who are shooting over there.' (They had heard the gunshots from where we worked.) Soon they were all stuffing it into their pipes. Everyone had a clay pipe of his or her own. Yes, men and women.

'Give Mary a wee puckle to make a fag, Daddy.' 'Better Mary would learn to smoke the pipe. They fags are not good for anyone,' he said—passing Mary enough for a couple of roll-ups.

After a few minutes I asked Daddy for a draw of his pipe. 'Just a wee draw, Daddy, to taste it.' He took the pipe out of his mouth, wiped the shank with a corner of his shirt and handed it to me. This although I was only eleven years old at the time. Travellers are very fond of tobacco.

'Come, wee woman, I think that should do you now.' 'If you filled a kettle with tobacco this lassie would smoke it to the bottom through the stroup, without a halt,' he said to the others. 'I always put my pipe and matches into my bonnet at the front of the bed at night, and I've seen her when she thought her mother and I were sleeping. She would creep cannyways over our feet and get the pipe and matches to light it, then put them back canny again after she had her wee draw. When she was only four years old!'

'Now if a body had a drop tea...,' Uncle Duncan said. 'Who's making the tea?' The tea had been forgotten in the excitement over the tobacco.

3

The fire they had made was just embers and the water in the big black can had nearly all boiled away.

Liza had made a well over at the corner of the field. 'Go and get some fresh water,' Father said and I went to do as he asked.

'Watch and no' burn yourself,' Liza shouted to me, as I went to get the black can. 'Do you think I'm silly?' I answered her. My mother had taught me the dangers of fire when I was still on the breast. (In those days they kept bairns on the breast long after they were running about.) I picked a couple of docken leaves and lifted the can from the fire, protecting my hands with the dockens. Then, throwing out the little water that remained in the can, I made my way down for fresh water—taking a cup with me to lift it in.

It was a lovely little spring. I wondered to myself how Liza could always manage to find water like this. She could be walking along the edge of a field, an old road or even a main road, and she would stop and say 'I think there is clean water hereabouts.' Then she would poke about with a stick and after a while lovely spring water would come bubbling up the stick like a fountain. Then she would dig with her hands, tearing away clods of earth and make a nice wee well, placing chuckie stones at the bottom of it. Soon the earth would settle down and you could lift the clean water.

This well was surrounded with watercress and already dozens of water spiders had found it. I marvelled at the speed with which these little creatures moved, darting out of the way of the cup as I lifted the water. Mother had often told me that they only lived on pure water.

Haws were hanging in bunches from a hawthorn tree. I must have still been hungry, as I pulled handfuls and ate them as I made my way back, spitting out the stones.

They had built up the fire again and were all sitting around it. The October sun had been warm while we worked but now, after sitting a while, you could feel the nip in the air.

Soon the water was boiling. Liza had made a big iron frying pan of skirlie ('toll' we called it) and was piling the skirlie on to slices of bread and handing them around. My other aunt, Bet, was dishing out the tea shortly after. She just threw the tea into the boiling water, lifted the can to the side of the fire then spooned sugar into it, finally adding the milk and stirred it up.

Mary had showed them the scones while I was away for the water. Four big thick scones cut into fours and spread thickly with home-made butter and cheese! They were shared equally.

'She must be a nice woman, that farmer's wife.' 'Aye, she is,' I said, 'and she has gallons of that beautiful skimmed milk.' It was my Uncle Duncan, Liza's man, who had spoken. He was my favourite uncle—tall, well-built and good-looking. Although his eyes were like indigo, his hair was black and curly. He never spoke a lot. He didn't need to as he could learn more from one glance than most people could in an hour's conversation.

'The country people are awfully stupid in some ways.' 'How, Uncle?' I asked. (We always said how instead of why.) 'Well,' he said, 'there is that farmer's wife. She will likely throw out all of that skimmed milk to the pigs and other animals. They think there is no value in it but, if they only knew, it is the best of the milk. The juice of the grass and herbs that the cow eats. The cream is only the fat of the cow.'

'If Hendry doesn't come, his wee drop tea is going to be stone cold.' Someone else was speaking. 'Where did he go?' I asked. 'He said he was going for a dander, but I don't think we'll see him again until the work is finished. I think the work was going to his butt.' This from my Uncle Andrew. 'Maybe he went back to his wife and bairns.'

'No, the lassie won't have him back. She has had enough of him. He was brought up in a Home, you know. Any bairn that is taken away to they Homes is never right. When he was about nine he was gotten standing at the door of an inn. His mother and father were in the inn. The woman wasn't drunk, but the authorities took the bairn anyway. She prigged with them, but it was no use. The woman broke her heart over her bairn and she died not long after that.'

Father's voice and the clink of our hukes were the only sounds, except for the wind and the birds.

'He would steal the milk out of your tea,' Father continued. 'He took my pipes the last time he came to us and sold them to old Hughie. Hughie knew the pipes, and he guessed that Hendry had stolen them. So he bought them from him, and came all the way down from Pitlochry to give them back to me. I still haven't paid the old man, but I will when these neeps are finished. No, no, I don't know what they do with the bairns in they Homes but I do know they are pure rogues when they come out of them. Hendry has been chased from camp to camp for his cockiness and his thieving. The other travellers will not hit him or report him and he knows that and lippens on it. Some day somebody will give him his tatties.'

I had often wondered why this man Hendry got off with the things he did. Any other man would have gotten a sore face and ribs for less. But they pitied him, having been in a Home, and at any camp that he came to someone would put him up and feed him. They even laughed among themselves at his exploits, but were glad when he moved on.

The women were talking away among themselves now but I was keeping close to my father's heels, more interested in the men's crack.

Daddy and I were very close. His two sons had died in early childhood with pneumonia brought on by whooping cough and, although Mother had had three more children after that, they were all girls. So I was as near to a boy as he could get—weaving baskets with him when he wasn't working and even learning to play the bagpipes. Girls rarely played the pipes in those days.

4

Dusk crept in like a cold stepmother's breath.

'I think we'll call it a day, boys.' Daddy was the oldest
and usually took charge. He straightened his back painfully,
and looked at me a look which I could understand. A look
which said 'You've done well, bairn, keeping up with the
men all day.' But when he spoke it was to tell me to go to
fetch his coat and to gather together the dishes and things
which we had left where we had made the fire.

Mary was much too sore to help me, for her body was
not accustomed to this back-breaking work. They were all
chaffing her about the way she was walking but admiring
her gameness at sticking it at all.

'I wonder if Katie's home yet,' Mary said. Katie was an
older sister and was about Mary's age—nineteen. Mary
missed her since she went away to live with my oldest sister
Bella, who had just had a baby.

When a traveller woman had a baby she was not
allowed to prepare food for at least a month. Some other
woman or girl usually did the cooking for the husband
during this time. Men just would not accept food out of the
hands of a woman who had had a new baby. So Katie was
doing this for our sister Bella, who already had three
children.

If there was no woman or girl to be got then the
husband would do it himself, cooking for his wife and
children. However, this was very much against the grain of
traveller men, who thought it very degrading to do any kind
of woman's work. So it was very seldom that another
woman wasn't available.

Bella and her husband were living at Alyth in a house,
because one of the bairns had been unwell. 'How long is it
since Katie went away?' I asked Mary. 'Five weeks come
Sunday?' 'Yes,' she said.

The laughing of children and the barking of a puppy
greeted us as we reached the camp.

We had a barricade up. This is a bit added on to the
sleeping quarters—but much higher, allowing standing

room. It was built with long sticks of hazel or birch and covered with any kind of covering to be had—old sacks, tarpaulins, or what have you. There was a hole left in the top centre to let the smoke out. The fire, often an old dup tin made into a brazier, was in the middle and we could all sit around it, sheltered from the cold.

Mother had been very busy. She had a huge pot of broth ready and another pot filled with swedes and potatoes, mashed together with a knob of butter and pepper and salt. Another pot full of boiled rice, to which she always added one or two beaten eggs, was also ready.

After our bellies were filled the men would lie back and smoke and chat, while the women got on with the rest of the work. Some went for water which had to be carried in pails—some half-mile easily. Others went to gather sticks for the fires. Sometimes the men would do this, but more often it was left to the women. Then there were the children to be washed and bedded, all the dishes and pots to be washed, and clothes to be washed out.

Mary wanted to do the dishes, but Mother didn't trust her with this chore. Although we often went about a bit ragged and even dirty, we were very particular where food and dishes are concerned. Travellers still are.

A big enamel basin was kept for washing dishes and dishcloths in. Nothing else was allowed to be washed in it. Food was kept in a box away from folks' breaths and if anyone coughed or sneezed over food it would have to be thrown away.

Mother had once broken two lovely little bowls because Mary had stepped over them. 'Have you no sense at all, lassie?' she had said. 'You don't step with your petticoats out over dishes. You could have lifted them up instead.' It had been some of the men who had left the bowls on the ground—had it been a girl or woman she would have been reprimanded for it, but men were different.

'You do the dishes, Bessie,' Mother told me. She knew that I hated dish-washing and waited for my rebellious reply. But I was still a bit worried lest the gentry would send a policeman or, worse still, a Cruelty man up because I had begged the tobacco. So I just went to do as Mother asked.

I heard her outside the tent saying to one of the others 'Bessie's surely going to die. She's actually doing the dishes!'

5

I was still a bit worried as I lay in bed that night.

So you can imagine how I felt when I heard someone bellowing and shouting at the screich of the following day. My heart was in my mouth with fear, and I wondered if I could possibly sneak out the back of the tent and run and hide. Father and some of the other men jumped into their trousers and went out.

It was the farmer—and he was boiling with rage. 'Which of you bloody tinker buggers stole Charlie's new bike?' (Charlie was the farmer's son who used the bike to go to school.)

'Bike, Mr Robertson? Nobody here would steal a bike. You should know that by this time. We've been coming here to do your harvest, tatties and neeps, for five years now. You should know us better than that.' Father spoke gently, but the farmer was not to be pacified.

'It was no other body but one of you. Nobody else knew just where it was kept—and you will all be out of here before seven o'clock, every last one of you.'

Mother whispered to my father in cant to ask him about our pay, but Father declined. So Mother spoke up for herself. 'What about our money for the neeps, Mr Robertson?' 'Money! Money!' He opened his mouth so wide, and bellowed so loud, I thought he was going to eat us.

Mother had risen so hurriedly that she only had on a blue blouse and skirt. Her hair, which was my father's pride and joy, hung down almost to her thighs. Usually she was quiet and mild in manner, but when she did erupt you might as well face the Devil.

'We are not leaving without our two or three coppers,' she said. 'You know fine that none of us took the bike. It's just an excuse to keep the money.' 'It's the police I'm going for,' said the farmer, 'if you are not out of here in an hour.'

'Well, better you hadn't, Mr Robertson.'

At this point Father interrupted her. 'Shaness, Maggie,' he said, 'never mind the money.' He knew what she was going to do, he also knew that it would be as surely as she said it. It frightened him a bit, I think.

'He deserves it,' she said. 'He could keep whatever the bike cost and give us the rest of our money. God knows we worked hard enough for it.' 'Not a penny do you get!' the farmer shouted.

'It's quite alright, Mr Robertson,' Mother said—very quietly now—'*but you needn't care what you do from this day onward*. Goodday to you.'

Soon the tents were all pulled down and our few possessions bundled up. The straw which had been our beds, and the camp sticks, and anything which we couldn't manage to carry, were all gathered together and put a match to and—when there was not as much as a caramel paper of dirt or rubbish left on the farmer's ground—we started down the old farm road. The women carried bairns, baskets and bundles, and the men were also laden.

Glamis Green was not very far along the main road, and when we came to it we all stopped and dropped our bundles. We were all ganting for a cup of tea, having had none that morning. So a fire was soon lit, water brought and the big black can singing.

By now they were all laughing at our hurried departure and the antics of the farmer and were joking among themselves about it. Of course they all knew that this had been Hendry's doing. They were sure he had taken the bike and, likely, sold it. He would probably be having a good drink and feed with the money. But there was no anger in their hearts towards him—although they swore his life when they caught up with him.

'Well, what are you all going to do now?' Father finally asked. 'I think, myself, I'll go back to the town and put the bairns back to school.'

We had to have two hundred attendances at school, by law. This was a hundred days. 'A hundred days too many for me,' I thought. But it had to be done, otherwise Father could be jailed and we children could be put in a Home. So, although my heart dropped at his words, I didn't protest.

Two of my uncles and their wives decided to stay on Glamis Green for a day or two. Uncle Duncan and Liza said that they would go back to Pitlochry and school their bairns. He wasn't very fond of Forfarshire. Mary and Johnnie were to go with his father and mother over the hill to Aberdeenshire.

Few eyes were free of tears as we went our different ways. The women gave each other earrings or brooches or whatever most treasured possessions they had. The men were doing the same: handing over treasured whippets, even offering their bagpipes, and blessing each other before taking their leave.

As we passed Glamis Castle, I kept looking over the dyke and wondering if it possibly could have been the Duke of York who had thrown the tobacco to me.

'I think we'll go up to Alyth for Katie, stay the night on Alyth Green and make our way down to Brechin tomorrow, Maggie.' 'I suppose there is nothing else for us.' Mother and Father were talking as we walked along. They both looked a bit dispirited now, missing their friends.

'We are doing well going without a penny in our pockets or a stitch of clothes to put the bairns back to school in,' Mother went on. 'Aye, Charlie seen to that,' Father answered. 'Ach, but God's strong. You never know what might turn up yet.'

We must have been a sorry sight as we walked through Kirriemuir. Father carried a huge bundle on his back, containing our bedding and the few bits of clothing that we possessed. Mother had a bag on her back with all our dishes, pots, and pans in it, and a basket on her arm—a big square basket. In it she had a few odds and ends of stock: needles, thread, elastic, bootlaces and other things.

'The bairns must be starving,' Mother said. 'If you keep the two wee ones here at the end of the town, I'll take Betsy. We'll go and take two or three houses, and try and get something for the bairns.'

So we left Father and little Nancy and Lexy. Mother and I went through the town, but luck was against us that day. Try as she might, she couldn't even get one penny.

After a couple of hours she was beginning to get irritable. 'God curse him with the mallet brows,' she said, and I knew she was referring to the farmer. I used to cringe when she started this cursing and muttering as I knew that it would probably end up in a fight between her and Father. 'I'm not a bit hungry, Ma,' I lied. She looked at me and, reading my thoughts, started to smile. 'No wonder, bairn,' she said, 'no wonder I am angry.' But she stopped her muttering and fuming.

We had just about given up the thought of getting anything that day when a lady shouted to us from the door of a big house. 'Would you come here a minute, please?'

Mother was a bit apprehensive as we walked up the short stone-covered drive. The woman was at the door waiting for us. 'I have some things which I wonder would be acceptable to you,' she said to Mother. 'Anything at all would be very welcome today, ma'am,' Mother said. 'We had a church sale yesterday and there are quite a lot of odds and ends left which you might be able to make use of. There is also some home-made jam and cakes and tins of this and that.'

'Come down here,' she said, leading the way to a shed in the garden. 'But how are you going to carry them?' 'I'll soon carry them,' Mother replied. Soon she was packing her basket with the beautiful home-made cakes and jam. Then she was packing the clothing into a big sack which the lady had given her.

'I might as well tell you, I have no money,' she told the lady, 'but if you are needing any of these small things....' 'No, no, I don't want anything, I just didn't want to see them going to waste. You are welcome to them.' I could feel Mother's sigh of relief. 'God bless you, ma'am,' she said. 'Have you far to go?' the woman asked. 'No, my husband is just near so I will manage alright.'

'Thank God for that,' Mother said as we walked down the drive. 'You run and get your father and watch the wee ones till he comes to help me.' I hastened to do her bidding, and when the two of them arrived back we children all started excitedly exploring the contents of the bag and basket. We were not disappointed. There were frocks, jerseys, shoes and other things—and if they didn't fit properly we would make them fit. And food a-plenty.

'I told you God was strong,' Father said.

That night we slept on the floor of Bella's house in Alyth, tired out after walking all day. Mother had persuaded a cottar woman to keep our bundles in her shed until we came back for them, taking only her laden basket with her. In the morning we children fussed over our sister's baby: we had been too tired the previous night. And we were pleased to see Katie again.

Bella's husband was working in the woods and he would not be pleased until Mother accepted money from him to pay our fare down to Brechin. He also gave my father an old bike with which to cycle down, collecting our bundles from the cottar woman on his way.

So we arrived back home to the little old house in a close, which we had spent the last three winters in. It was only one room, but we managed. Mother had a constant fight with the fleas in it and—as her only weapons were paraffin, carbolic soap and water—it was a losing battle. Our skin used to come up in large blotches with their bites, for we were all very fair-skinned.

Mother resented very much having to live in this flea-box all winter. She would have much preferred living outside in a barricade. None of her people ever lived in houses. Father's people, on the other hand, had always housed up in the winter time.

'Never mind, Maggie, I'll take you away as soon as the yellow is on the broom,' he would say. 'Next year we will go up to your side of the country.' (Mother's young life had been spent in the Highlands.) 'Aye, you are good at promising,' she would say. 'But this time I will, Maggie, I promise you.'

6

On Monday morning it was back to school for Lexy and me. (Little Nancy was only three.)

I hated it, especially as there were no other traveller children at it for us to play with. The other children avoided us and taunted us continually and we were not allowed to sit on the same seat as a 'country' child. Of course we were behind with our lessons, but most teachers more or less just suffered us in their classes. I was in the Qualifying class now, and the teacher was a man.

One day he asked me, and another girl who sat in the seat at my back, to come out. 'Look at these exercise books,' he said. 'This is the third time this has happened, and it is too often to be coincidental. Both these sums wrong, and both identical. One of you must be copying.'

This girl piped up 'It is Betsy, sir. She is always looking round copying off me.' I was stunned. Apart from not having enough interest to be bothered copying, I would have needed a neck like a swan to manage it. Yet her word was accepted without question.

'I will have to strap you, Betsy.' I said nothing. I never did at school, having long before found out that it was useless. The schoolmaster took his strap out of a drawer and said 'Hold out your hand.'

As I held out my hand I heard the girl who had accused me, and some of the others, tittering. At this I felt all the suppressed venom welling up and the rebellious pride, which I had inherited from my mother, rose in me. I withdrew my hand just as the strap descended. It caught the teacher with some force just below his knee. Then I gave him two sharp kicks on the shin bone and fled out of the room.

Unfortunately the headmaster was just making his way to our room and he caught me in the corridor. I was shaking from head to toe and unable to answer him. I suppose I was really in a state of terror.

He led me by the arm back to the class where the young teacher, his face fiery red, was just trying to overcome his astonishment at my behaviour. 'What has happened?' the headmaster asked. 'That ... that ... girl!' the teacher replied, suppressing what he really meant to call me. 'She refused to take the strap and actually kicked me on the shins.'

I felt more composed now, somehow feeling a comfort in the headmaster's presence. 'Is this true, Betsy?' 'Yes, sir,' I replied. 'You know this is a very serious affair. I will have to deal with you myself. Come with me down to my room.' I followed him quite meekly. I couldn't care less if he strapped me a hundred times—as long as it was out of sight of those sniggering children.

On reaching his room the headmaster seated himself on his chair and looked up at me. 'Now then, Betsy, tell me all about it.' 'The girl behind me blamed me for copying, sir. I've never copied in my life. Then her and the others started making a fool of me when I was about to be strapped.' 'You didn't care much for that, did you?' he asked—then surprised me by saying, before I could answer, 'Neither would I.'

He then reached into a drawer. For his strap, I supposed. But instead it was an exercise book that he took out. 'Sit down, child,' he said, handing me the book. He then started to ask me a lot of questions about sums, spelling, and asked me to write down what I thought were the answers. He then gave me mental arithmetic.

'Well, Betsy, I think you could prove to Mr Arbuckle that you don't need to copy—if you would just try.' Not quite understanding his meaning, I asked 'How, Sir?' 'By doing as I tell you. Come back to my room when school is finished and I'll give you some books. Now off with you back to your room, and tell no one that you didn't get a walloping. I'll come down with you and talk to Mr Arbuckle. But remember, if you ever kick a teacher again you won't get off so easily.'

After school the headmaster gave me books which explained how all the sums we were getting were done, and one which explained grammar. 'Study these at home,' he said.

This headmaster was the best thing that ever happened

to me. He taught me how much one can learn from books, and I became very interested in them. I would lie down and read to my mother and father at night. They would listen enraptured. Mother used to buy those twopenny weeklies we used to get, and waited impatiently for the next instalment of *The Red Barn Mystery* and other favourites of the time.

One day I found an old book in a dump. *Three Men in a Boat* it was called. If you had been passing at the time I was reading it aloud you would have wondered what in the world we all found to laugh so much at. (Of course there were libraries, but we never thought that they could be for the likes of us and we wouldn't dare to go into one.)

I really did improve at school too—much to the delight of the headmaster, who really took an interest in me and gave me confidence and encouragement. He implored my parents to stay in the town until after the Qualifying Examination for secondary school. I didn't let him down either, being one of the three in my class who won bursaries. He told my parents that he would pay what else was needed for me to go to High School, as this bursary only paid for books or something. I didn't quite understand it.

Poor headmaster! He was pestered and bullyragged by irate parents who were convinced that my getting a bursary had been his doing. As it had in a way, but not in the way that they meant. How was it possible for a tinker child to pass and not their child? They wouldn't believe the poor man that the examination papers went to Forfar and that he wasn't responsible.

7

But it was the middle of June by this time and the yellow would soon be falling off the broom.

So Daddy wasted no time getting out of the town.

We had wintered well and he had saved enough to buy an old yoke. Katie had been working dressing potatoes and Father made baskets, with a little help from me. He used to take me on his bike and we would leave the bike hidden while we walked up the bank of the river Esk to where he had his willows growing.

Yes, *his* willows. He had planted most of them himself just by cutting some branches and sticking them here and there into the ground where he wanted them to grow. He tied the top of each in a knot so that it would sprout from there. They had to be cut every year otherwise they would have grown into trees. He used to tell me not to let anyone know where they were, lest any other traveller would go and cut his 'wans', as he called them. He would tie the willows on the back of his bike and set me on front, going home.

The willows then had to be boiled and the bark peeled off. He would stand them upright in an old dup tin filled with water. The upper parts he swathed in old sacking, tying it around the willows. (He had an old wash-house to work in.) When they were boiled he would call us all out to help peel them with sticks he had made—shaped like a clothes peg and called slipes. He would sit and tell us stories and give us guesses while we helped to slipe his wans— passing his pipe around.

He had no difficulty at all selling his baskets, as there was a woman called Lady Maitland who lived in Edinburgh. She used to visit us about twice a year, bringing blankets and sometimes clothes with her. She arranged for Father to send all his baskets to her and she sent him a postal order back for them. I think she put them into shops and sales of work. He received one and sixpence each for them. Not a lot, but it saved Mother walking miles trying to sell them. This Lady Maitland did a lot of good work for travellers and also for many other underprivileged people. She devoted much of her life to this work.

There was also another lady in Perth, Lady Hardy, who did the same. She was true blue and understood travellers better than anyone would believe possible, visiting them and helping them in more ways than I can describe. When any traveller got out of his or her depth she could always be relied on to help. Such was her understanding of us that she might have been almost like one of ourselves—if you can understand what I mean by that. A truly wonderful person.

19

I don't know if they were really titled ladies or not, but we always called them Lady Maitland and Lady Hardy.

8

But to get back to my story.

There we were, on the road at last: but for my headmaster, we would have been away in April—or May at the latest.

We were to stay at the 'tea and sugar' camp that night. This was an old road about four miles east of Forfar—quite a good way to go in a day at that time. Mother and I walked, Katie used Father's bike and Lexy and Nancy sat in the float. Father just let the pony clip-clop along at its leisure.

We were bound for Speyside, where Father would pearl-fish the river until the raspberry-picking started at Blairgowrie. (We would get no turnip-thinning this year: it was too late now.)

There was a family of McDonalds and one of Lindsays on the 'tea and sugar' camp. Father and the other men soon got together for a news and a game of quoits. Mother and the other women got together to exchange all the things that had happened since last seeing each other—and of course there were always plenty of children for us to play with.

Travellers simply adore children and to them no fate could be worse than being childless. Such couples were greatly pitied and more than often a sister of either the woman or man would give them one of their own children to rear. Of course the child was told, and was pleased in a way, because it knew that it would be lavished with anything that the couple could possibly get for it.

All travellers spoil their children. They rule the roost from the minute they come into the world. Young mothers seldom take offence at grannies, aunties, cousins or any other relatives for taking a part in—and enjoying—the rearing of their children.

Many a young wife received a beating from her

husband if her child got hurt badly in any way or had an accident. For some obscure reason they seemed to *like* their husbands to beat them for this. They would almost proudly show off a black eye or other bruises, saying 'That's what I got from (mentioning the husband's name) because the bairn burned itself (or hurt itself).'

This, and their love for their children, made them very vigilant. It was a very rare thing for a traveller child to be burned or seriously hurt—although they were always around open fires, rivers and on the roads a lot.

Yes, the children *were* all spoiled. Me along with the rest.

That night we all gathered round a big fire and had a sing-song, singing in turn all around. 'Tell a story, sing a sang, show your bum or awa' ye gang' was what was said. So everyone did their thing, long into the early hours of the morning, smoking and drinking tea all the while. We children usually fell asleep listening to them.

Next morning we were up and on our way again after prolonged goodbyes.

Our next stop was at the railwayside near Alyth, near the golf course. There were families of Stewarts and Higgins on this camp, and their company was so good that my parents stayed four nights there. Of course they spent a lot of time with Bella and her husband, who decided to come with us to Speyside.

The Stewarts were a very musical people and accordions and pipes rang every night. Father took a delight in making me play the pipes to them—and I took even more delight in the praise and flattery I received.

So in this way we made our way up to our destination, meeting and enjoying the company of other families on our way.

9

When we arrived at Speyside, Father made preparations for his pearl-fishing.

Pearl shells lie almost submerged in the sand of the river bed and are very difficult to see. Many pearl-fishers just waded out into the river and used a small glass-bottomed 'jug' to see the river bed more clearly. But Father used a boat and a jug almost six feet long. His chances of finding a good pearl were much better, as the deep water was rarely fished.

First he brought some wood and made a boat, flat-bottomed. It was shaped a bit like a snow-plough and he tarred it to make it waterproof. There was a flat plank— really the seat—along the inside of the boat.

Then he made the long jug. Some travellers made their jugs themselves with tin, but Father had never learned tin-making. So he got an old friend to make one for him and he put in the glass bottom himself. I can remember him snipping around the glass with a big ordinary pair of scissors. He put the glass into a big bath of water and kept it under the water while he snipped it down to the proper size. He said that this could only be done under water.

The jug was narrow at the top and widened out at the bottom, with a handle at one side. Melted candle grease was used to make it waterproof and melted lead was added around the edge of the glass to keep it upright in the water. The bottom of very deep water could be clearly seen through one of these jugs.

Last, he made a pearl stick. This was a long stick split at the end with a little wedge in the middle.

Daddy used to lie on his belly on the plank in the boat and, with the jug in one hand and his pearl stick in the other, peer at the river bottom for hours on end.

To bring up a mussel, he pressed the split end of the stick down on it and gripped it firmly. Holding the jug in his mouth, he pulled up the stick and took the shell from the end of it.

While Father fished, Mother had the task of keeping us all supplied with food. The little money which Dad had saved was all spent by now. Katie looked after Nancy and Lexy and I went with Mother to the houses. In the evenings Dad and I would make a basket each for Mother to sell. We cut the willows at the river side. (They don't need to be boiled in the summer as they peel in their own sap.)

So Mother would have a hard task this week or two. As we went from cottar to cottar, farm to farm, she would talk to me all the time; telling me about her parents, who were long dead, and about her sisters and brothers. Mother had fifteen brothers.

10

One day as Mother and I were going through a stack yard to a farm we heard this awful commotion and, rounding the corner, we almost bumped into the farmer.

He had a pitchfork in his hand and was chasing a big black hen, bellowing at it all the while. Between his roars and the squacking of the hen I was terrified. 'Come here, you black devil-riddled creature!' he was shouting. But the hen took wing and landed on top of a big haystack, opened its beak and let out a loud cock-a-doodle-doo.

'Do you hear it?' he shouted at us. 'Do you hear that?' and there followed a string of oaths directed at the hen. 'Aye, I hear it alright,' Mother answered him—but she just kept on walking, with me clinging to her arm. The last that I saw was him throwing the pitchfork at it.

'Moich cowl!' (Mad man!) I said to Mother. 'No, no, lassie, the man is not mad. Did you not hear that hen, what it was doing?' I must have looked puzzled because she continued. 'Did you not hear it crowing like a cockerel? A hen that does that is supposed to bring terrible bad luck to the place. The folk here are superstitious and a lot of them are Highland.'

'The crowing hen and the whistling maid
    should never be seen in any farmyaird.

'Have ye never heard that rhyme?' she asked me. 'No,' I said. I hadn't even noticed that the hen was crowing. What I mean is that I thought it quite natural for a hen to crow—never having paid any attention to the difference between the noises cocks and hens made.

We reached the farm door, which was open. A woman

was standing, turning the handle of a churn, the sweat running down her ample face.

'Oh, no, no!' she cried. 'That's all I need, for two of you kind of folk to come in-about!' She threw herself down on a stool, put her head in her hands and started stamping her feet one after the other, rocking herself back and forth at the same time.

I was ready to take flight but Mother gripped my hand tightly and stood her ground. We had walked far for absolutely nothing and we were both very hungry and tired. So Mother was getting a bit desperate.

'God bless me, woman,' she said, 'things must be going awfully against you today.' 'You can say that again,' the woman replied. 'The maidie is lying ben there, no' able to walk. She was kicked with a cow and I've been churning this damned thing for hours, but the butter will not set, and what with that devil's hen running through the place and now you two.... I am sure it was that bloody new vanman that brought the bad luck to the place. He had an eve going every road.'

'I hardly think so,' Mother answered her. 'The poor man can't help the eyes that God gave him. If it is anything at all it is more likely to be something within yourself. Something on your own conscience, woman.'

I thought the woman was going to explode. She jumped up from the stool and came forward. Mother still stood her ground and kept looking her in the eye. The woman faltered and said 'Of course, you kind of folk ken things.'

'Aye,' Mother said. 'We ken things and I'll have less of this "you kind of folk." I am just skin and hair, flesh, bone and blood the same as you are, and before very long you will be just a handful of dirt the same as I will. Go try your churn now, or let me do it,' she said.

Passing the woman and grabbing the handle of the churn, she began turning it. Soon she was needing all her strength to turn the handle.

'Damn my skin!' the woman said, 'but it's set already!' 'I bring ill luck to nobody's door,' Mother told her. 'You will have your butter ready for tomorrow's market and nae bother.'

'You are surely not very much acquaint with gan-aboot people,' Mother continued. 'Well no, you see, I....' 'You have been a nurse,' Mother interposed, 'and you were late in getting married, but you come off farming folk.'

'So you have the gift, have you?' The woman was a bit awed. 'Gift you may call it,' continued Mother, 'but it is more like a curse to me. I more than envy those who are not tormented with it. It would be heaven for me to be free of it.'

At this point the farmer came round the corner of the doorway, carrying the ill-fated hen by the legs. Its crowing days were over.

'There's a fine supper for you,' he said, dumping it at Mother's feet. 'No, praise be to God, it wouldn't go into my mouth,' Mother told him. She was not above superstition herself.

'Get it out of here!' his wife shouted to him. 'Take the bally thing away well without the precincts of the farm and bury it or, better still, burn it!'

'Well, we'll be on our way,' Mother began, but the farmer's wife said 'No, no, you are not getting away like that. Come read my fortune for me.'

Mother was not very keen on fortune-telling for gain. Somehow she felt that it would be using her gift as black art and putting herself in the clutches of Satan. However, she complied with the woman's wish.

She took us in to her big kitchen, which reeked of good wholesome food. A large roast lay on a marble-topped table with cakes and scones, trifle and lots of other goodies.

Only then did I realise just how hungry I was. My stomach whammelled inside of me and it was more than I could bear. I rose to go out again, saying 'I'll wait outside for you, Ma.' But the woman restrained me. 'Sit down, dearie, and I'll give you a piece.' Within minutes she had a bowl of milk and a large piece of still-warm dumpling set before me.

I was too entranced by my surroundings to pay any attention to what Mother was telling the woman. Everything was so spotless and beautiful. The big black range and the brass knobs on it were shining, as were the brass fender and toaster. There was a huge Welsh dresser on which were displayed numerous willow pattern dishes. My father had told me the story of the willow pattern. The tablecover where I sat was of the most exquisite embroidery that I had ever seen. A jug, with the Selkirk Grace on one side and a picture of Burns on the other, stood full of milk.

As I sipped the milk and ate the dumpling I wondered how on earth people with such an abundance of everything could go into such a panic about butter not churning or a hen crowing. It would have to be real bad luck to take all this away, I thought.

Even the little bowl that I drank from was rimmed with gold and decorated with roses inside and out. The floor was of stone whitened with cam—but not too much—with rugs here and there. On one side of the fire there was a case packed with books. They must spend quite a lot of time in here, I thought. How I would have loved to open that bookcase and take my pick of those books. And this was only the kitchen! What wonderful wealth of possessions there must be in this large house! I was truly overawed.

Mother's voice, saying my name, brought me back to earth. When I looked, she was preparing to go—well laden with whatever the woman had given her. Mother was pressing the woman to take the two baskets from her. 'They will be very useful for your eggs,' she insisted. 'Not unless you let me pay for them,' the woman said. 'Payment enough I have here,' Mother replied. 'I want nothing for telling your fortune.' The woman gave in before Mother did, accepting the baskets and bidding us goodday.

The ploughmen on their horses' backs passed us as we went down the farm road. 'It must be after five o'clock,' Mother said. 'Your father will think the Devil has taken us—and we have three miles to walk to the camp.'

'Never mind him, Ma, you must be starving. I'll go to that cottar and get them to make some tea for you. I've kept a bit of dumpling for you.' 'No, no, bairn, eat it yourself. I can wait till I get home. I have plenty food in my basket here.'

When we got to the camp we discovered that another two families had moved in—two of my mother's brothers, who had heard that we were there, and had come to join Father pearl-fishing. Father was helping them put up their tents. They were my uncles Jimmy and Hendry and their wives Nellie and Bell, who had nine children between them.

Father liked Mother's people, but not their fondness for drink. This had come about because they were quite good pipers. Any ploughman, gamekeeper or other man who liked a drink himself would give one to a wandering piper or fiddler. For some odd reason, others would rather give a wandering piper a dram instead of a copper or two. So my uncles became much addicted to John Barleycorn and every time they got a few shillings together they would get drunk.

I do not mean to imply by this that all Mother's relations did was to play their pipes and drink, for they worked very hard on farms. But Father discovered that it is never much fun living in the company of hard drinkers if you don't take it yourself.

11

Father had stopped drinking when I was six years old, on the day of his mother's funeral. (He had been a heavy drinker before then.)

I can remember it so well: all the carts and horses lined along the road outside the little cemetery at Caputh. We children stayed in the carts while friends and relatives from near and far attended the funeral.

Afterwards most of them made their way into Blairgowrie and, as was their custom, went to get drunk. The yokes were left in the Wellmeadow, with an older child—or at least someone—in charge. Our Aunt Nancy, Mother's sister, was the one chosen to look after our yoke, her two children and my sister Lexy and me. Whisky and beer were carried out to her and we children got biscuits and sweets.

As darkness fell, Aunt Nancy made a bed in the bottom of the cart for us. It was a high-spring cart. She cooried the four of us down, warning us for the peril of our lives not to make a noise or get up, lest anyone should see us and know we were there. 'Now you know what will happen if the police or "Cruelty" sees you,' she said, 'so not a sound.' I must have slept, because the sound of someone climbing up on to the cart woke me.

It was Johnnie Whyte, my uncle, who was married to one of my father's sisters. He seated himself on the rail at the side of the cart. Now this Johnnie Whyte was an off-taking, impudent blowhard of a man. My father and his brothers could have murdered him at times but he had no relatives — and they would never dare to hit a man who was just himself among them, with nobody at his back.

Lying there on the bottom of the cart, I heard the souch of them all returning. As they got nearer I knew that there were arguments going on, and it went from bad to worse. Women screaming, men shouting, swearing and the thumps as punches landed — but we children lay still like mice.

Then Aunt Nancy was in the driving seat. I caught a glimpse of her hand lifting the whip, heard it go crack-crack above the horse's back and felt the cart take off with a sudden jerk. As it did so, Johnnie Whyte — who had still been sitting on the rail — overbalanced and fell off. The last I saw of him was his legs disappearing over the side of the cart.

Arriving home, I heard someone ask Nancy if the rest of them were coming. 'They have all been stardied!' she answered. They were all in jail.

Next morning all of them were freed except my father, who was held in custody. Mother was going out of her judgment with worry. She had been told that he was being held on suspicion of having given Johnnie Whyte a paggering. Johnnie was lying in Perth Infirmary unconscious, not expected to live.

So for the next three days Mother couldn't be bothered with anything. 'I can't tell you a story tonight, bairns.' 'Wheesht, bairns, my head's splitting with your noise.' But she did sing us to sleep: mournful old Gaelic songs that made us glad to escape into the unconsciousness of sleep.

In the early hours of the fourth morning I heard a sound which made me jump out of bed over to where Mother lay. I shook her and shouted to her to get up. 'Listen, Mammie, listen!' There could be no mistaking that whistle. No one, nowhere, could whistle *The Shepherd's Crook* so beautifully —but Daddy! We threw something on and ran out barefoot. Sure enough it was Daddy and we three girls ran out to meet him, shouting 'My Daddy! My Daddy!' He dropped on the grass and let us romp all over him.

That evening I heard him tell Mother that he would never put strong drink in his mouth again. Taking out his Bible, he swore it on the Bible. And he never did put strong drink in his mouth again until the day he died.

'If Johnnie Whyte had never regained consciousness and told them that he had fallen from the cart, I might have been hanged,' he said. Johnnie Whyte recovered.

So Father was always on nettles when he lived among Mother's folks. When they drank, that is, and that was at every possible opportunity. They played their pipes to all foreigners and holiday-makers who loved to visit this beautiful part of Scotland. So they were seldom sober.

Every evening there was drinking, dancing, pipe- and accordion-playing, singing and, finally, fighting.

Father used to take a canny walk to himself when the fighting started. Not that he couldn't have held his own with any one of them and, anyway, they would never have touched him when he was alone amongst them. But we couldn't stand the sconcing and jibing they gave him because of his abstinence. They used to persuade Mother to drink with them and this added to his discomfort. So he would come wandering back after they were all exhausted and sleeping.

In every other way they were the nicest people imaginable and would share a nut with anyone. They had no regard for money at all other than to get rid of it as quickly as possible. To keep something for the next day never entered their heads. They could go without food for days on end—as long as they had their tea and tobacco.

Yet they were big, well-built, strong men. My mother told me that they had once capsized and fettered a farmer's bull when they were half-canned. (The farmer had a notice up telling everyone to beware of the bull!)

They were so high-spirited and fond of their freedom to

29

shout, sing or get drunk that they mostly stayed in isolated places. But they knew how to conduct themselves when they had to mix with the country people.

12

As the days passed, more and more of Mother's brothers came to see their sister Maggie, so Daddy spent more and more time in his boat.

The Spey is a very deceiving river: the water being so clear that it is difficult to judge its depth. So the children were kept well away from it and I was refused permission to go with Daddy. But he made a swing for us in a wood which spread down to the right of our tents.

One day when a crowd of us were playing there, climbing trees and eating wood sorrel (I had long before learned the things which we could eat) I noticed the strangest thing. Tiny little frogs were all over the leaves of the tree my cousin and I were climbing. Two or three of them could be on a leaf without their weight having any effect on the leaf. Then I noticed that they were coming down with the light summer rain, not thickly nor quickly, but now and again at intervals—like spiders on their silk. Jessie, my cousin—who was about my age—even managed to catch one as it came gently down. Soon we were all gathering them and setting them all over us. Wee Nancy and Lexy had them lined up their arms and ran to let Mammie see them.

Mother was busy making dinner and was surprised that we should make such a fuss about the frogs. 'Have you lassies never seen a shower of puddocks before? God bless me, bairns! I thought you would all have kent about that.'

Yet I have never seen one since.

I ran to meet Daddy that evening, asking him if he had ever seen a shower of puddocks. He assured me that Mother was right but couldn't tell me how they got up there or where they came from.

'Nae luck yet, Daddy?' I asked. 'No, just a few seeds,

nothing worthwhile,' he answered, 'but I have three crooks in my pocket for your mother to open.' Crooks were big crooked shells, like an old boot, and were the ones most likely to contain pearls. Father always liked Mother to open his promising-looking shells, as she was lucky at opening them. Some people are luckier, he said.

Pearls are a peculiar stone and can even be temperamental, changing their colour on certain people and becoming a dull, dirty, bluey or grey colour which makes them valueless. Pearl fishers have often been disappointed at this: finding a beautiful clear pearl, then discovering that it lost its colour within hours. But with Mother it was different. They got more beautiful every day in her possession and some discoloured ones even regained their beauty.

We always had dinner in the evening—as it was the only time that everyone was there—and afterwards Mother opened the shells, with us all gathered round her. Indeed one of them did contain a good pearl, a perfect pear-shaped drop.

Daddy's eyes nearly popped out.

'Maggie,' he said, kissing the hair at the top of her brow, 'this is a miracle! Remember I told you that the jeweller in Perth had asked me repeatedly for a pearl drop like this? Aye, I'm sure that is the right size and colour too. Lady Hogarth wants him to make a pair of drop-earrings for her. He has one drop-pearl but couldn't get another to match it. I'm sure this one is as near as he'll ever get, and I'm just as sure that he'll give me a good price for it. Two years he's been searching.'

My mother's brothers were very pleased when he showed them the pearl. They hadn't done much fishing. It was too slow and unrewarding for them, but their pleasure in his find was genuine. There was no envy in their hearts.

Material things had no attraction for them: only enough for their immediate needs.

13

Father was not materialistic either, but he loved to give pleasure and happiness to others, helping anyone who was down.

His worst fault was that he forgot that charity begins at home. He would buy a yoke for one of his brothers, give another money to tide him over a bad patch, and so on— leaving poor Mother with the heavy end of the stick to carry when the money was done.

I think it must have been the way that they were brought up. A man's word was law and women were supposed not only to keep them but to serve them hand and foot.

My sister Bella's husband was different. He was what we call a buck—half-traveller, half of the country—his father being a country man.

He wouldn't let the wind blow on his bonny Bell. She *was* bonny, too. Venus would have envied her figure and she had eyes like Daddy: large and vivid blue flecked with gold, deep-set like little china cups. She had inherited Mother's beautiful chestnut hair and was altogether as nice a specimen of woman as I have ever seen.

Her husband worked, if he could find work, giving her all that he earned. When not working he took a tip from travellers and could often beat them at their own game: buying writing pads and going round with a bike selling them. He wanted Bella to do nothing but look after the place and the bairns.

He would get up in the morning and give Bella a cup of tea in bed, then heat the baby's nappies and other clothes at the fire before handing them in to her. If he had any spare money he would take her into a town and tell her to buy clothes for herself. He would even baby-sit and let her go to a cinema, and wash out nappies and things while she was away.

The traveller men derided and chaffed him continuously, but it was like throwing water on a duck's back. He ignored them. I often heard them talk among themselves about him. 'What man would sit and watch bairns and let his wife go gallivanting to a cinema?' 'Did you see him washing hippens the other night?' 'Aye, and getting up giving her tea in bed.' 'I doubt I would be pulling her out by the hair of the head, and giving her a good kick into the bargain.' Daddy even talked like this about his own daughter. But Willie, her man, never ruffled his feathers but continued spoiling his bonny Bell.

One day we noticed a big open car draw up. A man stepped out of it, jumped over the dyke and started walking towards the tents. He was a dark, impressive-looking man and—as the men were all away and most of the women also—we were a bit apprehensive. We children scattered like rabbits: some to the wood or bushes, others hiding inside the tents.

Bella would have hidden too, but it was impossible with two tiny toddlers and an infant. So she had to stand her ground, even though she recognised the man who was coming towards her. To add to her terror, his first words were 'At last, at last, I've found you!'

He then proceeded to try and persuade her to be his assistant. He was Doctor Boddy, who had noticed her in town and had been scouting the countryside looking for her. Of course he had known that she was a traveller from the fact that she had been barelegged and with her hair hanging loose down her back. Only travellers went about like that in those days.

I was cooried inside her tent and could hear every word he said. I hadn't wanted to desert her in case he was a 'shan gadgie'—an unpleasant man looking for a woman. I had my father's whittle in my hand in readiness. I knew where he kept it hidden during the daytime, and I wouldn't have hesitated using it if he had attacked her.

(A whittle is a heavy knife with a handle, something like a butcher's chopper. It was used for cutting camp sticks, but its main use was for protection against Burkers or any other intruders. All the men had one and it was kept near at hand, just under the straw at the front of their bed—and heaven help any intruder! All travellers were aware of this and whistled or spoke, to let themselves be known before entering, if they came in-about late at night.)

However, I didn't need the whittle. He wouldn't believe that she was the mother of three children—nor would he believe that she could possibly refuse the tempting offer he was giving her. If only he had known! 'I shall return in the evening when your parents are here,' he told her as he left.

At the sound of the car engine starting and moving off, I came out of my hiding place to find Bella out cold on the ground. 'Water, quick!' I was shouting to the other children. I soon got a jug of water but hadn't a clue what to do with it. I knew better than to pour it into her mouth. Her two toddlers were screaming their heads off. Lexy and Nancy and at least a dozen other bairns were crying and asking 'What did he do to her? Bella! Bella!'

Bella stirred and came to herself just as my aunts Jean and Nellie came running in-about. They had been away for water but on hearing the noise of us they had known something was wrong, so they left their pails and rushed back.

On being told that Doctor Boddy had been there I thought that they were going to pass out too. You see, the word Doctor always struck terror into the hearts of travellers. They abhorred doctors, believing them to be something less than human. No human being could kidnap and cut up another human being, they thought—firmly believing that doctors spent most of their time doing this. They knew for certain that some doctors did this, and classed them all the same. They knew that one or two of their kind had landed up on a dissecting table and that quite a few had had narrow escapes.

Of course they were forced to attend doctors sometimes. They would never risk a child's life by neglecting to seek the aid of a doctor—their own life, yes, but not a child's. When a really old person was taken to an almshouse, as they sometimes were when it was impossible for their families to manage any longer, they never lived very many hours. Indeed, even many a middle-aged person, suffering from pneumonia or other serious illness, passed away shortly after admission to an almshouse. I am sure that most of them died from sheer fright. This, of course, made the others twice as terrified to go into one of these places, believing that the others had been done away with. 'Given a blue pill' was the expression used.

So you can imagine the pandemonium in the camp that day.

Bella was sent to look for Father on the river, taking three of us older children with her. Luckily, we soon found him. He immediately jumped on his bike and hurried into town to try and round up the rest of the men.

The women were another problem but usually they all came home about three or four o'clock at the utmost. Meanwhile we pulled down the tents, packed our few belongings into our respective carts or floats, burned all the rubbish and were ready for the road.

The women began to trickle home and when Mother came she gave Bella a good lashing with her tongue. 'Do you see what you've done now with your gallivanting? What married woman would run about like that? I've told you a hundred times to get that hair pinned up with hairpins, but I would be as well speaking to that cow over there! What have I done to deserve such stupit bairns?' And so she went on. Poor Bella.

It had taken Father quite a while as the men had all been at different places maybe about a mile or so apart— but, as one usually knew where the others were, he eventually got them all homeward bound. Those who had been fairly drunk soon sobered up at the mention of Doctor Boddy's name.

There was no time for prolonged goodbyes and soon we were on our different ways. We headed back towards Blairgowrie for the berry-picking.

Mother knew all the old byways, which had once been main roads but were now little more than tracks, and we followed these. Bella and the bairns were on our float as they didn't possess one. Willie, her man, walked beside Father as he led the pony by the head. Mother always preferred to walk and at this time Bella was glad of this. She knew that Mother had not finished with her.

'Have you any tea and sugar, Maggie?' Father shouted back to Mother. 'Aye, but no milk,' was her reply. He pulled the pony up and started to gather sticks to light a fire, saying 'Send those two young women to look for milk,' meaning Katie and Bella.

'I'll have to get milk, anyway, for my baby,' Bella said. 'Oh aye, aye, of course.' Mother had just been waiting for an opening to start on her. 'You are not fit to be a mother. That poor wee lamb of a bairn gets a big lump of rubber stuck in its poor wee mouth, and cow's milk. Your bairn will grow up to have the nature of a beast because you are too lazy even to feed it. I tell you it will be incapable of feeling true affection, even for you and its father.'

At this point Bella's husband spoke up. 'Don't blame Bella, Maggie. I persuaded her to put this one on the bottle—and it was me that took her to see Doctor Boddy.'

Mother didn't spare him either. 'Oh, as if I didnae ken, blue buck, as if I didnae ken.' (For some reason bucks were always called blue.) 'Well, you should think black burning shame of yourself.' 'Bella is my wife now, Maggie, you have no business with her.' 'What's that you say? No business, eh? No business with the bairn I bore out of my own ribs and reared tenderly up to womanhood? I tell you now, blue fella, that I will take business until the day I die if I see any of my family gan agley. Now get on that bike and don't come back until you get milk for that infant.'

Mother had never before interfered. I am sure it must have been the sight of the infant sucking at an empty bottle. 'Look, Bella,' she said, 'now what if there was no milk to be gotten? You know that I only want what is best for you, lassie.'

'Wheesht, the two of you,' Father interrupted. Something could be heard coming along the road.

It was Mother's brother Hendry and his wife and family. 'I tracked you to here,' he said. 'I have heard so much about this berry-picking at Blairgowrie that I thought I would give it a try.' Hendry and Ina had six children and one girl, Jessie, about my age. We were good pals, and I was glad to see them but I doubt if Father shared my pleasure. Hendry was one of the habitual drunkards, but Daddy welcomed them anyway.

Willie returned with the milk and after a bowl of tea, and a share-out of whatever there was to eat, they sat cracking and laughing at themselves. 'We are a brave lot, aren't we? So many of us running away from one man?' 'I wonder what he thought when he came back and couldn't see the picture of a soul about the place?'

'He reminds me of the Devil, that Doctor Boddy,' Ina said. 'When did you see the Devil?' her husband asked her. 'I ken fine he looks like the Devil,' she retorted. Nearly all the men had seen Dr Boddy as he travelled from town to town.

They would have laughed more at themselves had they known that Doctor Boddy was only an entertainer. It is unlikely that he was a doctor of medicine at all: he probably used that name because it sounded mysterious and awe-inspiring. He wore a long black cloak and a lum hat, and looked very sinister. I had often seen posters of him. He could make his pretty girl assistant float about in the air, and suffer a high voltage of electricity to go through his body—or seem to.

So they discussed him for a while with awe in their voices, then Hendry asked all about the raspberry-picking. They had never been as far down the country as Blairgowrie, for they preferred the Highlands of Perthshire.

We didn't bother putting up any tents that night. We gathered rushes and grass to make beds on. Bella lay with her baby cuddled in her arms. All traveller women did this, and never have I heard of one being smothered—although I have seen babies sucking away at their sleeping mother's breast. Yet the mother would awaken instantly if the baby coughed or was sick or struggled for more space. So Bella's infant was cosy enough although we had no tents up.

(We were not allowed to call the baby his name yet because he had not been christened, and it was considered unlucky to call a child by name until it had been christened.)

14

Four days later we arrived at the place we were to pick berries at, about three miles from Blairgowrie.

There were not many travellers at this farm, but there were rows and rows of bell tents in a field occupied by 'country people', mostly from Glasgow. The farmer always gave us a piece of land to ourselves, away up the side of the berry fields. There we pitched bell tents lent by the farmer instead of our own. We children and young people were given strict orders not to go near the tents of the scaldies (the lower-class town dwellers) as many of them were sure to be hotching with vermin, consumptive or—worse still— have the shan trouble.

We were taught to fear contagious diseases and Mother was an expert at diagnosis. When we were going round the doors, she very subtly got to know whether there was any dangerous illness in a house before taking anything from the occupants.

On the pretext of being very interested in the welfare of the occupants she would question the woman of the house. 'Well, how is the world treating you these days?' 'And the bairns, are they all well and healthy?' And—although she had seen nobody as she approached the house—'Was that fine-looking man I saw your husband?' Whereupon the woman would give her the details of her family. If Mother was satisfied that all was well, then she would go ahead and beg whatever she needed. Before leaving that house she would enquire about the house or farm that she would be going to next. And, although she had perhaps never been there before and hadn't a clue who occupied the house, she would say 'Is it still Mrs McLauchlan who stays up the road, the poor soul with the delicate man?' On this the woman would give her information about the occupants of the next house.

However, if Mother could have seen the people she would have needed no information about them. A glance was all that she needed to tell if a person was consumptive or disease-ridden, mentally retarded or had a want. She often astounded us with the accuracy of her diagnosis—from the colour of the skin, the shape of the hands, the movements of the hands, and a person's eyes. People with a want were the most difficult but, within a very short time, Mother could know in what way they had the want—and humoured them accordingly.

So although we older children would have loved to join the numerous pastimes enjoyed by the Glasgow people, we dared not. Jessie and I used to watch their activities from a distance. Every night they would have concerts and barn dances. Others played Housie and two young men ran the Housie school. They really enjoyed themselves—singing, laughing, joking, well into the early hours of the next morning. They were truly a nice lot. Most Glasgow people are.

Uncle Hendry did not pick berries. He preferred to take his pipes and go playing them in town—usually coming home at all hours well canned, and awakening the following morning in the horrors of drink.

Now every morning the berry-pickers would walk up the side of the field where we camped. There was an old road they could have gone up but I think curiosity brought them up by our tents. They would speak to the ponies and dogs and to us, of course, if we happened to be there. However, the rattle of their galvanised berry buckets always struck a raw nerve in poor Uncle Hendry's sore head, and this was very annoying for him.

One morning he could stand it no longer and, jumping up out of bed, he said to his wife 'I'll bet you that I'll make them that they'll never come this way again, just in two minutes.' He knew that they were nearly always women. So he ran out of the tent, stark mother-naked, with his privates in his hand, and raced at them shaking his privates at them. Then he ran back into the tent again.

But little did he know of the character of the Glaswegian. Instead of running away screaming, they shouted to their pals (or 'chinas' as they called them) 'Ho! Jeanie, Sarah, Edna! Come up this way and see this!' 'Ho, mannie! Come oot and dae it again!' 'Come on oot again, mannie!'

We were all away out picking berries when this happened. When we came back at dinner time he was all packed for the road and Ina, unable to suppress laughter, told us what he had done. 'I wouldn't stay here another night if you were to give me all that every berry-picker in the field makes,' Hendry said. 'If this is your berry-picking you can keep it for me.'

As the usual goodbyes were said, I felt a bit depressed. I was going to miss Jessie very much. Sisters were alright but somehow Jessie and I were sort of soulmates. We got deep pleasure from the same things and activities, and never rankled on each other's nerves.

So for the next few evenings I consoled myself playing my practising chanter and reading a book which, unknown to my parents, I had asked from one of the Glasgow girls. It was *Gulliver's Travels* and I used to go away some distance from the tent to devour it, lying on my belly—listening to the cracking of the broom peas as they burst open, the humming of bees and wasps and sometimes a mouse singing in the grass.

One evening they were all looking for me. I had forgotten about time and it was my father who found me. 'Are you not afraid, lassie, lying there all by yourself? Mother is going her dinger. I'll have to make some kind of excuse for you. Come and we'll collect some sticks.'

Soon we arrived home, Father with a huge bundle of sticks on his back. 'The bairn was away gathering sticks,' he said to Mother. 'The next time you go anywhere for so lang, I'll break a stick over your back!' Mother shouted at me. 'How could you be so stupid, lassie, with so many queer kind of people wandering around at this time of year?' 'We got a book,' Father lied. 'We'll get her to read a bit of it to us tonight.'

'What's it about?' Mother asked and, when I told her 'Giants', she asked me to start reading then and there. Although she was highly intelligent, she was like a child for fairy stories—really enjoying them.

15

Father's pearl was burning a hole in his pocket or, rather, Mother's pocket—as that's where it was kept.

This pocket was enormous, shaped like a large horseshoe and made of tartan decorated with pearl buttons. She had made it herself, lining it with red taffeta. It had two compartments and was slotted at the top to allow a narrow leather belt to go through. The belt was fastened round her waist and the pocket hung down under her apron. All the traveller women made these pockets for themselves and kept any little treasure that they possessed in them.

'Do you think I should go into Perth with the pearl tomorrow, Maggie?' 'Please yourself. You've been ettling to go ever since we came here—but I want some of the money to get boots and clothes for the bairns going back to school.'

He got a good price for his pearl and—as the jeweller would rather part with jewellery than money, which was very difficult to come by in those days—he came home with a beautiful earring and brooch set for Mother. The brooch was mounted with three gold sovereigns and the earrings were sovereigns too. He also had a gold watch and chain for himself and hooped earrings for Bella. I don't know how much money he got but he bought presents for us girls too.

16

Soon the berry season would be finished, and Mother asked Father where we would go to the potato gathering that year. 'We can't go back to Robertson's farm,' she said. 'He will not have us back again.'

Father looked very intently at her. 'Maggie, I doubt Mr Robertson will not be worrying about potato-pickers or anything else this year.' 'Oh!' she said, her face blanching. 'Maggie, I want your solemn promise that you will never put the bootchlach on anyone again.' 'I can't help it!' Mother exclaimed, genuinely upset. 'I don't really want any harm to come to anybody, but I can't keep control of myself all the time. I wish to God I had never been born with it.'

'Who told you about the farmer?' she asked. 'My brother Jimmie, more than a month ago. He was thrown from his horse and broke his neck, but I kept it from you as I know how you feel about these things.'

Mother was crying now. 'The Devil must be with me,' she sobbed. 'He must have a hold on me somehow.' For the next three days food never passed her lips. She just smoked and drank tea, wandering about all the night and lying down, but not sleeping, during the day. Father tried everything with her, but she was curse inconsolable. So he did the only thing he knew would be any help to her—bought a bottle of whisky and doped her with it at night.

Mother's misery affected all the rest of us. Me especially, as I was—and still am—very susceptible to atmosphere. My laughing, lilting, singing, happy Mammie! How I wished that I could help her.

My wish was granted. I had long since finished reading *Gulliver's Travels* and had taken to reading my father's Bible. Although he couldn't read, Father always slept with the Bible under his pillow. If any of us was ever troubled with nightmares, he would put it under our heads. Not only Father but many traveller people do this, for it is a sure cure for nightmares. Daddy's nightmares had started when he came home from the war.

I had started reading the Bible for want of anything else to read, not understanding it very well. One evening, about a week after Mother's shock, I came upon the passage about Elijah and Elisha—reading and re-reading it. 'Mammie, Daddy! Daddy, Mammie! Listen to this!' 'What is it, lassie? Away and play yourself instead of sitting about like an old granny.' 'But just listen,' I said—and began to read the passage to them. Soon they were all ears, and had me reading it over and over again. 'You see, Mammie,' I said, 'Elisha was a man of God but the children were killed with wild bears when he put a curse on them, so you could just as easy be a woman of God.' Mother definitely picked up after this, but I read about Elisha so often that I can still quote it from heart.

Soon we were a happy family again. I think when the mother is happy the whole family is happy. When they are very young, that is. Little Nancy and Lexy who had been very quiet and biddable, soon became their boisterous, impish selves again. Katie, who had been meekly doing all the chores—well nearly all, I had helped a wee bit— regained her high spirits and let me know that I must do more in future. Bella could be heard diddling and crooning to her infant again. Willie her man, who had walked about for miles with his two wee toddlers, could be heard laughing and teasing Bella again. Daddy tuned up his pipes and we had a wee blow on them, with him correcting my mistakes.

17

'What do you want to do, Maggie, now that the berries are finished?' I heard Daddy ask Mother the following day. 'I would like to stay here for a day or two to get myself gathered together again,' she answered him. After a shock, time of worry, tension or frustration Mother always liked a few quiet days to 'gather herself together', as she called it.

Father scouted around on his bike and found a farmer who needed help with his harvest. Then, as we were a bit weary of our own company, he went to where his brothers Jimmie and Andy were and persuaded them to come too.

Andy was married to my mother's only sister; Jimmie, the youngest of Father's family, had married a 'country' lassie. Two of his sisters had found her, late one cold winter's night, sitting in the Wellmeadow in Blair. She had been heavy with child and absolutely destitute. Her father, a widower, had put her out of the house when he noticed her condition. She was only sixteen at the time. Granny had kept her, had seen her through her trouble and eventually Uncle Jimmie, Granny's son, had taken her for his wife. I had learned this from listening to my mother and the other women cracking. She was a neat, clean and industrious wee person and now had three children.

Annie, the oldest girl, was born the same year as I was.

She was a beautiful girl with no resemblance to her mother at all. She had a carriage and bearing which made her stand apart from the rest of us. She could put any old clothes on and look like she had stepped from a bandbox—and I had to chasten myself severely to keep my envy at bay. But I liked her and copied her a lot. She had a peculiar birthmark on her upper arm, shaped almost perfectly like a black swan: not risen, but smoothly on the skin. Granny had told Uncle Jimmie when he married Edna that he was never to cast up the child to her, nor question her about its father. She didn't need to tell him to be good to the child, knowing that he undoubtedly would adore it, as he did its mother.

So we shifted to the farm we were to work at. It was a bit isolated, between two villages but easily two miles from the main road. Uncle Andy and Aunt Nancy were already there and had a cosy wee place built. She had cut stacks of broom and made a shelter all around with it. They greeted us warmly.

'Come and see what I've got,' Uncle Andy said to us children. Round the back of his tent he had built a big square covered with netting wire. Inside was a hare, which rose on its hind legs to greet us. 'Come on, Rundy, do your stuff!' he told it, whereupon the hare started to beat a tattoo on a tin can which was in its enclosure. 'I found it when it was a wee leveret,' he told us. 'Its mother was caught by a dog. I used to sit and hold its two front legs in my hands and beat gently on the tin with them. He soon learned to do it himself and he follows me around like a puppy.'

Next day Uncle Jimmie and Edna arrived. Edna couldn't acquire the traveller women's knack of carrying their babies on their backs or on their arms, so she had her weeks-old baby tucked up snugly into a large basket which she carried on her arm. She had tried to buckle her first baby on her back but it had fallen right down on to the ground. Luckily, it was unhurt but she got such a fright that she gave up trying—yet in other ways she was almost like a born traveller. She had her own pipe and could go to the door with the best of them.

Traveller women vied with each other when they took

the doors, making themselves proper beasts of burden. I have seen some of them with a big child in their arms, a bag of old clothes, rags or what have you on their backs; likewise another bag with oats for the pony, a large square basket on the other arm and a can of milk, tightly lidded, gripped between their teeth. The basket might be packed with heavy dishes, together with all the food they could come by. They would walk home thus laden for miles.

Although the men of my father's and mother's people worked, there were other breeds of travellers whose menfolk never did a hand's turn, depending entirely on the women to keep them. They would scoff at men who worked, saying 'Women must be scarce when you can't get one to keep you.'

Although Father and his brothers worked, I doubt very much if they would have worked to a boss for very long, or even for a full six months at a time. I have often heard them say 'The country folks are all so silly. They start to work at fourteen, or even earlier, and go on working right up till they are old men, never taking any enjoyment to themselves.' Few fates seemed worse to a traveller than this. Most of them were good workers, and few men could beat them at any kind of piece-work—as long as they felt they were working for themselves.

But to work for a boss? Oh no, that was beneath their dignity. I've often heard such remarks as 'The big greasy farmer came in-aboot in a flash car, stepping out curling his moustache and shouted at me to get on with it. Me, the cold sweat running down my brow and my stomach croaking with hunger. No, no, I told him to stick his hay in his backside'—but that is not the word they used.

18

The men helped each other to put up the tents, after they came back, with the long hazel sticks which they had cut. They newsed and cracked, joked and played games, as they worked; making bets with each other as to who could carry the heaviest boulders to put around the tents on top of the tarpaulins. These bow tents were very cosy and could withstand the toughest gale that ever blew.

I remember one time, when I was about six, we were camped beside a wood near Kirkmichael. I don't remember what time of year it was, but there were five or six families of us working at cutting down bracken.

Anyway, we were not long in bed one night when a terrible gale got up—the like of which I had never heard before or since. 'Up with youse, as quick as you can, bairns! Hurry before we're all made in atoms!' It was dark inside the tent and everyone was groping for something to put on. I could hear zinc baths, basins and anything that was kept outside, rattling against trees and against the fence.

Once Daddy had lifted a corner of the tent door, which had been secured with a heavy stone, the force of the wind was too strong for us bairns to get out and it was impossible to speak. I felt Mother grab me and throw me over her shoulder. Then she was trying to get her plaid over me as she held on to my legs with one hand and also hold her eight-months-old baby on the other arm. I don't know how long she fought the wind like this before she put me down, peering to see was I alright, still gripping my wrist tightly. Then she turned her attention to the baby lest it should be smothered, as she had been forced to cover its face with her plaid.

We were out of the reach of falling trees now, but huge branches were hurtling past us in the wind. I could see Daddy a bit in front of us and I was sure that something had hit him as he was stumbling, crawling and falling every time he got up. He had Katie in one hand and little Andy in the other. I could see Daddy's two white hips in the semi-darkness and, as there was something trailing about his feet, I thought his trousers had fallen down.

The wind was choking me as I felt Mother throw me over her shoulder again. I don't know how she managed to get there, but next time Mother put me down we were at the other side of the moor beside a deep dry ditch. I felt Daddy pull me into the ditch. 'Are we all here?' Mother asked. She was pulling us to her to make sure we were alright.

Then she shouted to Father 'You are a clever man, you could have been over here with the weans and back to help me.' Father was giggling and laughing. 'Maggie, no wonder I couldn't do anything—I've got my legs into the arms of my jacket!' Soon we were all laughing at Daddy. A huge branch of a tree hurtled right over our heads as we squatted in the ditch, bringing the laughter to an end. 'God have mercy on man,' Daddy wailed, 'we are all going to be blown into eternity.' 'I'll put you into eternity very quick,' Mother said, 'if you don't stop frightening the weans. Don't be feared, it's only a wee blast of wind, weans.

'You will have to give me your skirt, Maggie, till I go and see if the rest of them are alright.' 'Aye, I'm going to give you my skirt, and me with nothing but a cutty semmit below it? And I cannot take the plaid off my bairn either. You will have to go as you are.' 'The plaid wouldn't bide round me anyway with the wind, but you could wrap it round you and the wean.'

Daddy was anxious about the others. Mother wriggled herself out of her skirt, hiding herself as she did so with her plaid. Daddy's bare hips had been on the ground as he sat holding up the back of his jacket in front of him. He pulled on Mother's skirt and rid himself of the jacket. 'Here, put that round one of the weans,' he said as he went crawling away along the ditch.

None of us had shoes on and soon we were all beginning to feel cold. We all cooried close to Mother. She tried, and somehow managed, to get all our feet under the plaid and we got the heat from her body. She told us tales of other wild winds twenty thousand times worse than this one and it didn't seem long till Daddy returned. He was hanging on like grim death to some heavy blankets which the wind was trying to drag away from him. After a struggle he got them into the ditch, then proceeded to make us all as comfortable as possible. He had his trousers on now, and Mother's skirt on top of them. He took some bread out of the pockets of it and gave it to us weans, just breaking it with his hands.

Mother knew that all the others must be safe, otherwise that would have been the first thing Father would have told her. 'Auld Eppie is still lying cosy, smoking in her bed,' he told Mother. 'She wouldn't move for her son Willie. Willie had to take his bairns to safety. He is worried to death about her; four of the tents are flattened with trees lying on top of them.' 'The old woman is wise,' Mother said. 'If she tried to fight that wind and lie in a cold ditch, she would probably die anyway. So she is as well worried as hung.' 'Aye, but Willie would be demented—and his wife too. One of them wanted to stay with her but she made murder with them, saying that she has had her day but they are young. I hope to God she will be alright.'

I must have fallen asleep and so did the other children. When I awoke all was quiet and it was daylight. Mother was sitting smoking. Then I saw Daddy's feet at the top of the ditch. 'Up, weans!' he shouted, and Mother pushed us up while he leaned down and pulled us out, and we made our way over to where the tents were.

Hardly a tent had budged with the wind. The canvas of one (which had been light anyway) had disappeared, others were flat with branches or trees lying across them, but three or four still stood untouched although uprooted trees were everywhere—even large beeches. Old Eppie had built a big fire and had about six cans and kettles round it ready for us to get the tea made.

'That was some night,' was all that she said.

19

I have wandered a bit, haven't I? It's funny how those memories of childhood come back to me so vividly that I can almost live them over again. Yet ask me what I was doing or where I was yesterday and I would have difficulty remembering.

Anyway, with the tents erected, the straw for the beds, sticks, water and milk brought in, we were soon all enjoying a cup of tea with the inevitable bread and skirlie.

The skirlie was nearly always made from the dripping off sootie pork—and was delicious. Sootie pork? The country folks killed their pig, salted it, cut it up into large pieces and hung it on the hooks attached to the rafters or roofs of their cottages. I know I often weary for a bit now. Nothing can compare with it for tastiness. The oatmeal, too, was a treat, almost like nuts, so our skirlie was not a soggy mess but crisp and really good. I used to eat handfuls of the oatmeal raw, or put a handful in a bowl of milk. Lovely!

When working hard harvesting or whatever in the hot sun, we were never allowed to drink water which did not have a handful of oatmeal thrown into it. This prevented the cold water from harming our sweating overheated bodies.

20

'Are you coming up to the bothy?' Uncle Andy asked Daddy and Uncle Jimmie.

Uncle Andy was strong, roguish, spirited and a bit sadistic—thinking nothing of coming round our bare legs with his steel-lined whip if we children got out of order. Jimmie was the sharger of the family, full of wit and always singing or making up songs and poems—mostly about the others. Daddy was more of a thinker: very diplomatic, with a good judgment of people and situations, completely unselfish, always thinking of the needs of others—physically, materially and spiritually. He lost himself in the need of others—but Mother was perhaps the exception. Whether it was her own independent nature, or whether it was the way that women were regarded in those days, I don't know, but it certainly was not for lack of love for her. Yet looking back now I realise just how hard her life must have been.

Traveller men nearly always went ceilidh-ing to the bothy when they were near a farm. They would play melodeons (few bothies were without a melodeon), wrestle, compete with each other at games of strength, tell stories or play cards.

The young ploughmen enjoyed those visits a lot. Poor creatures, they had so little enjoyment in those days. Up at five in the morning and out to groom and feed their horses;

then in again taking turns to make the porridge, which was practically all they lived on. Then out to work with their horses—really work—from dawn till dusk with perhaps a brose or another plate of porridge at dinner time and the same again in the evening. They got about six or seven pounds for a full six months' work and usually went into the nearest town and blued the lot at the feeing market. Occasionally they would treat themselves to a loaf and butter from a van, or perhaps one of their mothers would give them a pot of home-made jam.

'Fetch my jacket, Bessie,' Daddy asked me. His jacket was hanging on a paling post and as I lifted it I noticed he had several packets of cigarettes and two ounces of tobacco in his pocket. These, of course, were for the bothy lads. He had asked me to get his jacket because he knew that whoever fetched it would see them—and he also knew that I would never tell Mother.

His eyes met mine as I handed it to him, but there was no need for words.

21

After the men had gone, leaving the women to get the things all sorted out, the bairns washed and beds made, Annie (Aunt Edna's and Uncle Jimmie's girl) asked me to go for a walk with her. 'I'll ask Ma,' I answered. 'Well, nae doon by the burn,' Mother said. 'The burn' was actually the river Tay just down from the little village of Spittalfield and about two miles from Caputh—but travellers always called rivers 'burns'. Mother knew that I could never resist paddling in water so she wanted to be sure that I wouldn't be tempted.

Annie at twelve plus was just beginning to develop and in such a beautiful way that I couldn't help being jealous. She moved with such grace too. How I wished that I could be just like her, but I was straight up and down like a pencil. She must have read my thoughts because she said 'What beautiful hair you've got! I wish I was fair like you.

Everybody calls me Blackie more often than Annie. Daddy started it, he has called me Wee Blackie ever since I was born.' Now among travellers, and especially our breed, anyone black was supposed to be evil or bad in some way. I had often heard them say 'Anyone so black as that cannot be good' or 'I never seen a black body good in my life.' By 'black' they meant black eyes, black hair and dim, dark skin.

I knew that Annie was trying to make out that she envied me and my heart went out to her. She is as good inside as out, I thought. I pulled the earrings, which Daddy had brought back to me when he had sold his pearl, out of my ears and held them out to her. 'Here, you can have them,' I said. Her pleasure was truly genuine—more, I think, that because of this act she knew that I had taken to her than for the value of the earrings. The wires were gold but the drops were big imitation pearls and as she put them on I could see that I had thought rightly. They suited her much better than they did me. 'You suit them lovely,' I said without any feeling of envy—nor have I felt envy toward anyone again, at least not that I can remember.

We were on an old road which led to Caputh. 'Will your mother not be angry at you,' she asked, 'for giving away your earrings? Or your daddy after him buying them for you?' 'Never,' I said truly. To give away something that you really liked yourself was considered to be the only way to give—and was also considered to be the easiest way to tell someone that you loved them, without the embarrassment of the spoken word.

We played leap-frog over some corn which was already stooked, eating some of the grains after rubbing the heads of corn between our hands. We also picked and cleaned the hairy seeds out of rose hips and ate the shells. She was talking about her mother.

'She is very strict and suspicious, you know. She always blames me for speaking to boys and accuses me of telling lies.' 'Never!' I said again, but with a different meaning. 'I like my Daddy best,' she said, 'even if he is not my real daddy. He takes me to the pictures sometimes and buys me sweeties. She was never allowed to hit me if he was there, but now when she gets his back turned she batters me with a shoe if I am only ten minutes late coming back from a shop or school or from anywhere. Daddy caught her at it not long ago and they had an awful row. "That's a bairn you're at, you silly scaldie bastard!" he said. "Just because you were a hot wee bitch yourself doesn't mean that the bairn's like that. You must have been at it at twelve years old yourself." He grabbed her by the throat and walloped her. " Edna, it's not often that I have beaten you, but I'm thinking about the bairn. You will make her into what you are accusing her of being. Have some sense, woman. If that's the way your father behaved, that's not our way. So never let me hear or see you at this carry-on again or it will be worse for you." '

'Oh Annie, that must have been terrible for you,' I said. 'She must be mad.' 'No, just stupit,' Annie replied.

We had entered the tiny village of Caputh by this time and we made our way to the bridge, standing looking down into the water. There is another little village called Murthly, quite near to Caputh, where there is a hospital for mentally disturbed people, and it so happened that a warden was taking a party of about thirty of them for a walk. They were coming our way—all men.

'Oh shaness, Bessie, I'm thrash,' Annie said. 'Come on and we'll run the other way. That warden could do nothing if any of them attacked us.' 'No, don't be silly,' I said. 'We'll just keep walking on the way we are. Don't look at them or speak to any of them. Just keep talking and walk past them as if it were just anybody else. I have often come this way with Mother and that is what she told me to do. She says that the poor creatures are suffering enough without us making them feel worse by running from them and, when I asked Daddy later, he said that Mother was right. They are mostly intelligent sensitive people who land up in there, he said, especially the ones that you see out walking. There are much sillier and much more dangerous people going about outside who have never had any sense to lose. How would you feel if people ran away from you in terror?'

Nevertheless I could feel Annie shaking as we strolled past them. This was her first experience of seeing such people and was to be excused. 'God bless us all,' she whispered. We had been told to always bless ourselves if we saw anything or anyone with anything abnormal about them, such as a mongol child or a bad disfigurement of any kind, or a freak or even a helpless cripple. 'Never stare at them or pass remarks about them, just bless yourself and them,' we were told. If a traveller happened to be talking about someone like that, he would always say 'God bless the mark,' and, if any small traveller child was heard laughing at such a thing, he or she was severely reprimanded.

'We have to go back that way,' I said, 'over the bridge except we wade the burn.' 'We are not wading the burn,' she said, looking at me and laughing, 'or I'll tell your mother. If we hurry we'll be over the bridge before they come back this way. We had better not doddle, it must be getting late.'

There were two cottar houses just over the bridge and, although it was six o'clock when we left the camp, I decided to ask the occupants for a book. 'Are you coming with me?' I said. 'Shaness! I don't think you should,' Annie told me. 'Ach, they cannae eat us,' I retorted.

We approached the door and I knocked. Whenever I looked at the face of the woman who opened the door I knew that I was to be disappointed. She had a narrow face, with eyes to match which darted here, there and everywhere, round about us, behind us, out on the road—in fact, anywhere except straight at us. 'No, I haven't any books,' she said. 'Where are you staying?' 'We are not staying,' I lied. 'We are on our way to Essendy, our folks are about half a mile on the road.' 'What's your names?' she asked. 'McKillop,' I lied. We had been taught never to give our names, or to tell anyone where we were encamped. 'Well, get going,' she said. 'Books indeed, a fine excuse! If I miss anything, I'll have the police after you!'

This always infuriates me: the assumption that all travellers are thieves. How this idea originated, I don't know. Real travellers take too much pride in their ability to get what they need without stooping to stealing. By outwitting a farmer or a businessman in a deal—yes, the men take pride in that, but stealing? A real traveller wouldn't even stay on the same encampment as a thief.

They abhor thieves more than anyone. Of course there are exceptions as there are in any society, but to class us all as thieves! And this idea persists. Well, it always infuriates me.

We knew that the woman would be peering out of the window after we left. So we decided to go back to the main road, walk up a bit out of her sight, then cut across the fields.

As we approached the tents, Annie asked me to come with her to face her mother. Aunt Edna was inside her tent feeding the baby. She took the child from her breast, stripped it expertly without ever exposing it, using a warmed flannel to protect it. She bathed it all over with her hands, without the baby ever being exposed, and had it dressed again in minutes. Granny had tutored her well, I thought. 'Well, did you have a nice walk?' she said.

'Can I get a shot of the baby?' I asked. 'She is beautiful, isn't she? I'll keep her warm.' I could hardly believe what Annie had told me about Aunt Edna. I took a woollen shawl and wrapped it round me and the baby, making sure that its nose was clear of any clothes or of the shawl.

As I approached our own tents, Mother and Aunt Nancy peered at me. 'I thought you were a strange traveller woman coming in-aboot,' Nancy said. 'How old is she now, Maggie?' 'Going on for thirteen,' Mother answered. 'The farmer wants some of us to cut out lying beds of grain tomorrow. Do you want to come out with me?' 'Aye,' I answered Mother.

So early next morning Aunt Nancy, Mother, Katie, Annie and me were out in the fields. We looked through the fields for patches which had been flattened by the rain and wind. Mother cut them with a huke while I gathered up the grain, made it into sheaves and stooked it.

We were all ill-clad for the job as the corn was soaking wet, and so were we before very long. Our feet were squelching but we were so used to being wet that it didn't bother us. The grass round about our tents was nearly always wet in the mornings. Nor did we bother to change when we got home, just letting everything dry on us. The men were all stooking in another field. They too were soaked.

'Do you want a wee draw to heat your jaws?' Mother asked me. 'Here!' She handed me her cuttie pipe. It was brown and well seasoned with age. 'I'm going home early to put you back to school,' she told me. 'I promised your schoolmaster. He says it is a good chance for you.'

22

Mother knew little of the horrors of school. We didn't tell her anything that would vex her.

'I don't think your father has a penny about him, and him after selling his pearl and also getting all the money we made at the berries. Yet he goes on about folk spending their money on drink! At least they get something for it if they drink it.' She herself was hopeless with money too—having no regard for it whatever. The result was that we wasted and destroyed a lot when money was rife and hungered and wanted when it was hard to come by. The next day was never even thought about and next week was a hundred years away. Daddy did try but, as I said, he was always giving everything away.

Mother didn't know about the embarrassment I endured when I went to gym. All the other girls had sandshoes and shorts but me, I had clog-like tackety boots, and my stockings were either doubled down under my feet or with my toes sticking through them. The gym teacher had asked me to take the boots off but I had refused. She was a young French girl and was always teaching us country dancing. So you can imagine what I looked and felt like, clattering up and down doing Strip the Willow or some other such thing.

This year it would be worse. The High School girls all wore uniform—green gym slip, maroon blazer, black stockings. I had seen them often. Then there would also be hockey sticks, tennis rackets, sewing material, knitting wool, and things for cooking. All of these had to be your own at that time, and if there is any person more cruel and sarcastic than the High School girls of that time I have yet to meet him or her. I never talked to Mother about these things, and it never occurred to me to darn my stockings. We were still very primitive, I'm afraid. At that time I considered the 'country hantle' to be some kind of God-like people who could do wonders that we couldn't do. I just didn't want to have to be with them in the way we were at school, or any other way.

'I don't want to go back to school, Ma.' 'I don't want to go back to that dirty wee dark hole of a house either,' she said, 'but I promised.'

That night I had difficulty in falling asleep. Then it rained. The patter of the rain on the canvas of the tent was such a pleasant sound—so soothing, almost tranquilising—and I thanked God for the rain as I dropped off.

Annie and I had become inseparable during that harvest season. I felt so sad and lonely as I watched her walking away behind her parents' cart, her bottle-black hair shining in the September sun, when the time came for us to go our separate ways.

Our hearts all sank when we entered the house in Brechin. 'Dirty wee dark hole,' Mother had said, and that's exactly what it was after the beauty and freshness of the harvest fields and the autumn woods which we had left. Mother's 'sparring partners' were out in full force to greet us. She cursed as she surveyed the risen lumps made by them on our legs, and the rest of her day and evening was dedicated to their doom.

Monday morning and back to school, spruced and scrubbed but minus any school uniform—and also minus any idea of how to do the lessons which the class I was put in were doing. One look at my little plump teacher told me that she was minus any sympathy, indeed minus any of the deeper feelings. I was just going to be one long headache as far as she was concerned. So I was pleased to learn that we had different teachers for different subjects. I ignored the sniggering, taunting and sconcing which the other girls dished out, and kept to myself as much as possible.

Of course I had to mix a little, like when we played hockey or tennes. I didn't like hockey. Every time I took the borrowed hockey stick in my hands, I thought what an ideal weapon it would make, and often had to restrain myself from using it as such. But tennis I excelled in. Here was something that I could get a wallop at. Biff, bouff, bowf! I was soon adept at tennis.

Lessons were not much of a problem either as my former headmaster tutored me in his own home two evenings every week, and his wife stuffed me with lovely cakes and lemonade after each lesson. The knowledge that there were people like them among the 'country hantle' made me feel happier and gave me a glimmer of hope.

There was no work to be had that winter. Katie kept house, Mother took the doors and Daddy wove his baskets. If we didn't get enough to eat it didn't bother us, we could do with it or without it. The less there was in the house the more we sang, laughed, played music and teased each other. Often when Daddy got a postal order for his baskets he would take us all to the pictures. Never bothering about the fact that he would have been better keeping the money for food during the coming days! Tomorrow was another day, but we were so happy. Coming home from school I felt like a fly would feel if someone released it from a spider's web. A completely different world.

Come April and I really got my bellyful of the High School girls of the early 'thirties.

One day when we went back into school after playtime, I was asked to come out to the floor—where the Head, my teacher and another gentleman were standing. They asked me if I had seen anything of a ten-shilling note. Oh, not again, I thought. On several occasions I had been questioned about missing articles—money, gloves, scarves, even coats. 'Jenny was foolish enough to leave the ten shillings in her coat pocket,' the teacher was saying, 'and it is gone.' I looked towards Jenny, and never have I seen such malevolence in the eyes of a human being. Certainly never in the eyes of any animal, and I had seen all of the wildcats, foxes, serpents and lizards which my Uncle Andy was so fond of taming. Why, I asked myself, why, why, why? 'Do you mind if we search you?' the teacher continued. 'Her coat is in the lobby,' Jenny and three or four other girls piped in.

I knew before they looked that the money would be in my pocket. So I darted through the door and flew like a swift out of that school over the high dyke across a football field, a field of winter wheat, a berry field leafless and bare, until I came to the bank of the Esk river. The tears were tripping me as I ran. I never looked back as I knew that no human could have caught me, such was the added ability that fury had given to my body. I also knew that I had condemned myself as a thief by running away, but I didn't care. If I had stayed I would have been guilty of an even worse crime—murder.

I threw myself down midst the whins on the river bank, not feeling their sharp spikes which tore into my arms, legs and body, and I cursed that girl. Never had I felt such venom in my heart for anyone. It almost choked me. Then I sobbed and sobbed and sobbed again until I fell asleep. I awoke feeling very cold, as I only had a thin sleeveless frock on and ankle socks. I had a very painful job of extricating myself from the whin bushes. I felt sick and shaky. 'Oh,' I thought, 'my poor Daddy and Mammie.' They would be worried sick about me. It was gloaming but I was terrified to go home.

But I had underestimated Daddy's knowledge of my natural instincts. I climbed the tallest tree I could find to get a better view of the road leading to the river, and of the path along the river bank. And there I saw him, looking so dejected, even in the distance, that I knew that *they* had been down to the house. I scrambled down the tree and ran to meet him. 'My bairn!' was all he could say as he cuddled me. No questions. No condemnations or rebukes. 'We will cut up through the fields. Your mother and sisters are demented with worry.'

The pain came when Mother was trying to clean me up after a cup of tea, a chunk of bread and a smoke. The whins had been merciless. Some of their spikes were still sticking into my skin.

Mother's face was as white as a sheet and she looked drained and shaken. 'We waited for you coming home,' she said, 'and when you didn't, I went up the street to look for you and I got the wildest fright that ever I have got in all the days of my life. A woman told me that a girl had been killed with a car, as she crossed the road, just after coming out of your school. Then I met two policemen who came right towards me. "We were just on our way down to see you," were their first words. I would have dropped at their feet had I not held on to a lamp post. I thought they had been on their way to tell me that you had been killed, but it was only about the silly money. What happened, anyway?'

I told them just as it had happened. 'You were silly to run away. Now they think that you really did take the ten shillings.' 'Mammie, it was just after playtime in the afternoon. I had my pipe and matches hidden in a hole in the outside of the dyke, round beside the football ground. I hid myself and took a wee draw, then climbed the dyke when the bell rang and went right back into the school. They had it planned, Mammie, I could tell. That lassie Jenny Valentine! God curse her from the bottom of my heart this day. She put it in my pocket, I just know that she did, Mammie. *God curse her again and again.*'

'Wheesht, wean, wheesht,' Daddy interrupted. 'Come and I'll buy you a book before the wee papershop shuts. Here is a shilling, come on.' I clung on to Daddy's arm as we made our way to the bookshop. 'What will they do to me, Daddy?' I asked. 'They'll do nothing to my bairn,' he answered, 'I'll see to that.' 'Tuppence will do for a book, Daddy. Keep the rest for something else.' 'Get sweeties for it, for the two wee ones,' Daddy told me.

In spite of having slept that afternoon, and of the ups and downs of the day, sleep came easily to me that night. Just as well, too.

23

I was awakened in the dead ceilings of the night by my father gently squeezing my fingers.

'Rise, wean, we are leaving this place.' Mother was getting Nancy and Lexy up. Mother, Father and Katie must have been busy while we slept, as the house was bare of necessities—dishes, pots, pans and clothing. 'Don't make a cheep now,' we were told, 'be quiet as pussies.' Daddy gathered all the blankets and went outside with them, while Mother saw to it that we were warmly wrapped up.

The pony was waiting patiently on the street, and we were quietly lifted on to the float. There was barely a sound as Daddy led the pony to the end of the town. He had put hoshens on its feet. When we were clear of the town, he stopped and lit the candles in his lamps, while Mother made a bed in the centre of the float for us, Katie as well. Then he pulled the hoshens off the horse's feet and jumped up on to the float. A tarpaulin completely covered all that was in the float right up to where our heads were, and anyone looking at us passing would think that only Daddy and Mammie occupied it. Have you ever travelled along being able to see nothing but the dark night sky and the occasional dim outline of trees? It gives you an eerie sort of feeling. So we slept, coorieing down into the blankets under the tarpaulin.

It was broad daylight when I awoke, and we had pulled in off the road, and were in the midst of woods. Father was giving the pony some hay, but I could see no sign of Mother. This particular wood had wide track-roads made for the benefit of woodmen. Jumping down off the float, I asked Daddy where we were. 'This is the crying woods of Alyth,' he answered. 'How are they called the crying woods?' I asked. 'Well, supposed to be years ago that a young bairn was murdered in these woods, and that to this day it can still be heard crying.'

Father was making a fire now. He had gathered some perfectly dry sticks, so that there would be no smoke, and had banked a circle of earth so that the fire couldn't travel outward and get out of control. 'Katie, if you cross the road and follow they bull trees up that path you will come to a wee burn. Then follow the burn about a hundred yards and you will come to a wee well that your granny made years ago. You will easy find it, there is a holly tree just behind it. I would go myself, but I'm feared that a spark might start a fire.' Daddy was keeping an eye on Lexy and Nancy, who were warming themselves at the fire, and didn't see the look which sprang on to Katie's face.

'Aye, if you wait, I'm going away up there for water to you, especially after you just telling us that these woods are haunted,' she said. 'Sorry but I doubt you'll have to go yourself, and I'll watch the fire.' Daddy, however, knew that a fire could easily be beyond her experience, so he wouldn't go, and tried coaxing Katie with a draw of his pipe. 'I'll go with her, Daddy,' I said, wondering why he hadn't suggested this himself. 'Well, nae lifting papers or anything off the road,' he said. 'Now haste with you.' So we lifted our water pail and a cup and made our way out of the wood, and across the road. Sure enough, there was a path up alongside the elderberry trees—bull trees, travellers call them. I don't know why.

'How does he not want us to pick up papers or anything?' I asked Katie. ''Cos you're always raking about among papers and books,' was the silly answer that she gave me.

We soon came to the wee burn, no wider than a ditch, but it was hotching with trout. I immediately ran down to it and started to guddle for them. And when I successfully landed one, I almost had a fight with Katie because she nearly let it wriggle back into the water again. 'I don't know how you could do that to the poor wee creatures, that is a haneyin' sin,' she said. 'Aye, but it's not a sin to eat them,' I retorted. 'That wouldn't be a sin would it?' I taunted her, knowing that she was very partial to trout.

Katie had beautiful, thick, curly, red hair, and the temperament that usually goes with it, but contrary-wise she was incapable of violence to any living thing. I was so used to guddling for trout and chopping rabbits and hares on the backs of their necks to put them out of their misery after the dogs had dropped them, that I just never thought about it seeming cruel in someone else's eyes. 'You go on and get the water, and I'll guddle here till you come back.' 'No,' Katie answered me, 'come with me.' 'God pity you, I suppose I'll have to.' 'You had better, split mechanic.' ('Split mechanic' meant a female who does things that should only be done by a male.) 'Shut up, carroty head,' I shouted at her.

Then I saw the bird, a big fat mavis, sitting on the path a few yards in front of us. When we were nearly on it, it flew off only to land a few yards in front of us again. When it had repeated this action three or four times, I lifted some stones and threw them towards it—not trying to hit it, only to frighten it away. But it persisted in this behaviour. 'Get, you unsanctified bird!' I shouted at it. 'If you don't, I will hit you!' 'Leave it, leave it alone, lassie.' Katie's face had paled. 'I'll kill it!' I almost roared. 'Dirty skittery fat mavis!' But the mavis kept up its performance, undaunted. Now you may wonder why we should be so perturbed about the behaviour of a bird, but this bird—behaving in just this way—was supposed to foretell the death of someone bearing our name.

We hurriedly, but with some difficulty, got the pail filled with water. The well was a bit overgrown and difficult to find. Then we hurried back to where the others were. Daddy took the pail out of Katie's hand and, looking at it, said 'You are the two cleverest lassies that I ever seen in all my life. You have been away for over an hour and have come back with no more than half a pail of water. We'll not be long in making tea, giving the horse a drink, and washing ourselves with that.'

Mother had been into Alyth shopping. She had cut across the golf course. She said nothing, for a wonder, but after we had a cup of tea and something to eat, she said to Daddy 'I don't like the dream that I had last night.' (It was considered unlucky to tell your dreams before breaking your fast.) Daddy didn't question her about her dream, for he had lived with her long enough to trust her interpretation of dreams. Nevertheless she related it to us. I will not tell you her dream lest any of you should dream the same thing, and go through the same torture wondering who it would be that would pass away.

We knew that from this minute we would be guarded every minute—and pampered in every way possible. We would all be so good to one another, until this death took place, lest it should be one of us. Katie told them about the mavis, and Daddy started to pace up and down. Everyone looked so miserable, that I just couldn't stand it, so I shouted at them 'God knows what you are all afraid of dying for, I'm not afraid to die! Just as well to die now as later, when we have to die anyway.' 'My God, what kind of lassie is that?' Mother said. 'What kind of hard unfeeling heart do you have, lassie?' Of course I knew that their own death wasn't in their thoughts at all. Their dread was for their loved ones. And they knew that my outburst had not been caused by an unfeeling heart, but rather by the opposite.

'Stop your carry-on. We must get out of here before the keeper or any of the forestry workers come. Get back into the cart again and we will all get cleaned up at Bella and Willie's house later.' Daddy was already getting the pony harnessed. I looked around at them, and truly we were a sorry-looking sight—what with sleeping all night with our clothes on and not, apart from Mother, having as yet washed ourselves. I was worst of all, after kneeling in the mud when I had been guddling at the burn. I looked at the trout, lying where I had put it on the grass, and wished that I had never killed it. No one would eat it now, indeed no one would eat very much at all during the next few days. The adults especially would exist on tea and tobacco. The children would get something hastily and impatiently prepared. Perhaps impatiently isn't the right word; Mother just wouldn't be able to concentrate on making food, or looking for it.

Soon we were all back into the float, and covered with the tarpaulin. We couldn't risk anyone seeing us in such a mess. They would more than likely send the Cruelty people after us if they did, thinking that we were being neglected. So we lay under the tarpaulin—with Katie in beside us, giving us guesses or telling us stories in an attempt to keep us amused, especially little Nancy and Lexy. As I lay and listened to the clip-clop of the pony's trot, I thought that it was taking us an awful long time to go about two miles into Alyth. When we did stop I could see no sign of Alyth. We were on hilly country. Father had changed his mind and headed up Glen Isla.

We clambered off the float and looked around. It was a nice place to camp—with a burn running through it, plenty of firewood, and hidden from the road by a wooded area. After the tent was put up, a fire was made and the tea and fried bread eaten by us children. We all helped as much as possible, as we knew that Mother and Father were very tired for lack of sleep. We had washed ourselves in the burn, but Mother heated a big pail of water to wash the small girls' hair. 'I doubt we will have to sleep on the bare ground tonight,' she said. 'I'm much too tired to go looking for straw.' Katie and I offered to go look for straw, but she was afraid to let us out of her sight. 'I'll get straw,' Daddy said. 'I saw a big soo of straw not far away. I'll nip a few bunches when it is gloaming.'

We went to bed early. Daddy always lay at the front of the tent, then Mother and little Nancy and Lexy. A separate bed was made for Katie and me at the back. We always managed to retain our modesty, no matter how many people were in one tent. We put on and off our clothes under a blanket or cover. I have often seen travellers who have lived in houses for years, and who by then had a room of their own, still dress in this way.

Next morning I arose early, wriggled into my clothes and crawled outside quietly, taking care not to step on anyone. I had slept fitfully after lying thinking that it was all my fault that we were all in this predicament. There was some tea and sugar in a covered box still on the float, but not a scrap of food and no money either, I was sure. The trees were all bare of fruit or berries, and the earth was bare as well. I thought about going looking for a farm, but didn't want to worry Father and Mother. Most farmers' wives always had something to spare in those days—potatoes, oatmeal, milk—and most of them were really very tolerant of us travellers, feeling that it was unlucky to turn us away if they really had plenty and to spare. I knew that Mother and Father had heard me rising. They would have heard a fly passing, let alone me.

We had used the burn water the night before. It ran from the hills, and Father had decided that it was clean. So I filled the tea can, lit a fire and made tea, and took two bowls of it to Father and Mother. 'Are you haunted, lassie?' Mother said. 'It is not six o'clock yet,' but they both got up shortly afterwards. 'I will just have to make two or three heather reenges for you, Maggie,' Father said. 'There is a coil of wire in an old quarry down there. I'll go and get it.'

There was heather growing all around us. I helped Daddy to look for the carlin-heather, which is the only kind suitable for making besoms or pot scrubbers. It was not of course in bloom, but I recognised it, as its roots are much longer and thicker. So I pulled it when I came on a clump, and Father cut it the proper length. He then tied the wire round a tree and pulled it straight, and commenced to make the reenges—pulling the wire tightly round them with the aid of the tree at the other end of the wire, snipping off the wire with pliers as he finished each scrubber.

He then made two heather besoms. They were made in three sections, each something like a very large scrubber. The three were then bound tightly together with wire, in the same way as the scrubbers, on to a long, straight, peeled stick—the handle. These heather brooms were used widely for cleaning out stables, byres, courtyards, doorsteps, and nearly every house had a heather pot-reenge. If we couldn't get the penny asked for a scrubber in those days, we could get something to eat, and this was better than money.

We had been away for nearly four hours, but little Nancy and Lexy were still asleep. Katie and Mother were washing clothes and had to hang them on to bushes to dry. 'You will have to make me some clothes pegs too,' Mother told Father. 'I didn't take any with me.' 'Aye, some other day, Maggie,' he said. Mother decided to take Katie with her that day, leaving me with Father and 'the bairns', as I was inclined to look on Lexy and Nancy now. 'If you want to go anywhere, Daddy, I can easy manage,' I told Father. He looked at me with a look which I could not fathom, and sighed deeply. 'I'll wait till your mother gets back,' he said.

'Can I go and look for a trout up the burn?' 'Well, don't go out of sight,' Daddy answered.

24

So I climbed up the knowes and braes which the burn ran through, gazing at the water all the time, until I came to a place where the water lilted over big stones. Trout often lie under the stones—or, rather, under the ledge of stones. Yes, there were fish here alright. So I lay on my belly on the bank of the burn, waiting and watching. Then I heard a sound behind me.

Jumping up, I turned around and was almost facing the biggest pair of knees that ever my eyes had beheld. As big as soup plates, they were. I staggered back almost into the burn and my heart jumped into my mouth with fear. I looked farther, up past an Ancient Cameron kilt, past a rough tweed jacket to a red bearded face and long red hair hanging under a broad balmoral bonnet. He must have stood at almost seven feet. Never had I seen a bigger man.

'Oh now, did I fear you, girlie?' he said. He knelt down. I was shaking from head to toe and my throat had gone so dry that I couldn't answer him. So I raised my eyes to his face—or what little I could see of it for hair—until my eyes met his. Then I slumped into relaxation. The eyes were hazel. Pure unadulterated hazel, without a fleck of green or amber, and I knew that this giant would do me no harm. I bent and scooped some of the burn water into my mouth, to loosen my tongue which was literally stuck to the roof of my mouth.

'Aye, I did get a bit of a fear,' I answered him, 'I didn't hear you approach.' 'No, no, you wouldn't have heard me,' he said. 'I was treading softly. You see, Charlie's in this glen and the damned redcoats are everywhere hunting him, and although I'm a Cameron they might think that I am one of Charlie's men in disguise.'

My brain went at sixteen to the dozen, hoping for a chance to escape. 'They will never catch him,' I said. 'I saw him take over that knowe up there about twenty minutes ago. Louping like a young deer, he was, but with your long legs you could catch up on him with nae bother.' 'Are you sure it was Charlie you saw?' he asked. 'Would I no ken Charlie?' I answered. 'Slim, good-looking and with beautiful golden curly hair. Tartan trews he was wearing.' 'Aye, aye, that sounds like him alright, and I have some food in here for him,' he said, pointing to a big fishing basket on his back. 'Then hurry, man—or he'll be away out of sight.'

He started as if to go, then for some reason changed his mind and came back to where I was again. I had been ready to flee down to the tent, but thought better of it. I would have to humour this giant of a man. I knew that he could catch me with two or three strides.

'And who might you be?' he asked. 'Oh, I'm really a nobody,' I answered. 'That's my dwelling place down there,' pointing to the tent some five hundred yards down the braes, and wondering how he would take that. 'Ochon, ochon, well, well, I suppose there is a purpose for everything. We are all Jock Thompson's bairns, eh? And you were trying to catch a trout, girlie? I used to do a bit of guddling myself. I think I'll have a go.'

So saying, he took the fishing basket off his back, laid it down and sat on his knees at the burn side. 'I can see that you ken the kind of places where you're likely to catch them,' he said. 'Stand back a bit, girlie, your shadow's on the water. You will frighten the fish away.'

I stood back as he told me. Somehow I was quite relaxed and at ease with this big man now. But, when he leaned over the water, I could see what looked like a miniature elephant's trunk hanging down below kilt level and I immediately ran back to his side again. 'Did I not tell you to keep back?' he shouted. 'I can't!' I almost shouted too. 'And why can't you?' 'Because I can see your caber when you bend over the water,' I said. 'Then turn your head the other way, girlie.' 'I did turn my head the other way, but curiosity kept pulling it back again.'

At this he threw back his head and his laughter thundered through the glen, startling all the birds in a nearby rookery. I even saw two rabbits scuttle hastily into their burrow—and they must have been more than a hundred yards away.

'Oh now,' he said, 'I could eat you, girlie, I could surely eat you.' I had heard Highland people talk like this before and this man was as Highland as a peat. So I knew that he didn't mean this literally.

'Man, man, you're good,' he went on. 'Now I am sure you have seen a lot more than that. You kind of folk just live through one another like rabbits, dozens in the one tent.'

'You are very much mistaken, Mister. We do not live like rabbits. It would be telling you, if your kind of people were half as decent and modest as we are....' 'Now, now, dinnae tak' the gee on me.'

He put out a huge hand in friendliness towards me, but I took a buck leap across the burn—barely making it, one foot landing up to the ankle in the water. 'Don't run away, girlie. No harm meant, none at all.' 'Who's running away?' I said. 'I'm only coming over here so that I don't have to look at *that* again.'

Then I heard the sound of voices and, looking down, I could see Daddy and the two weans making their way towards us. Daddy had had me under observation since I left the camp. I knew that, and I supposed he was wondering who I was talking to. When they drew near I said 'Cor, Daddy, that's some climb, isn't it?' (This word 'cor' is a cant word and was thrown in to let Daddy know that the man with me was a bit unbalanced but harmless.) 'Aye, it's some climb alright,' he said, eyeing the big stranger.

Daddy looked dejected, and little Nancy and Lexy looked peeked and pale. They must be starving with hunger, I thought. My own belly thought that my throat had been cut, so what like were my two wee sisters? 'This is Mr Cameron, Daddy.' The big man stood up, dwarfing Daddy, and put out his big hand. 'Man, I am pleased to meet you,' he said. 'That is some girl you have there!' 'Aye, she's all that,' Daddy answered.

My eyes fell on the fishing basket. Did the man not say that he had food in it? I must get it, I thought. The look of my two wee hungry sisters had damped my spirits. The big man was talking to Daddy, and we had been told never to butt in or interrupt when adults were talking, especially to the 'country hantle'. But for once I was going to take the risk and do a lot of things I had been warned not to do.

'Daddy, did you bring me up anything to eat?' I interrupted. The look he gave me would have sunk a battleship. He didn't answer, but made a sound as if clearing his throat. A sound which I had heard often before, and which meant a reckoning for me later. He wouldn't hit me. He never hit us, but he would make me feel terrible, by showing how hurt and disappointed he was at my behaviour.

I could see that Cameron was really enjoying the conversation with Daddy, and was anxious that it should continue. So I shouted loudly 'Daddy, are you coming home? I must have something to eat.' Daddy started making apologies for me, but this time the big man had caught on. 'Here a wee, girlie, bring that basket over and I'll see what Kate has put in it today.'

Avoiding Daddy's eyes, I ran and lifted the basket. Whatever was in it was heavy enough, I thought. Big Cameron opened it and lifted something wrapped in a snow-white cloth. It was a huge cooked hen. Another cloth contained two cooked rabbits, and a stack of scones and sandwiches emerged from wrapped newspapers.

'In the name of the God, where were you going with all that food? I ken you are a big man but there is enough there to feed a battalion.' Before Cameron could answer Daddy, I stuck my tongue in. 'Oh Daddy, he fetched it to give to Charlie.' 'Charlie?' Daddy echoed. 'Aye, Prince Charlie,' I said. 'He is somewhere in this glen just now, isn't he, Mr Cameron?' I even had the gall to look innocently up into the big Highlander's face as I said it.

Daddy drew in a long slow breath, as he waited for Cameron's reply, because up till now Cameron had shown few signs that he was 'away with the fairies', as we called it. 'Yes, yes, man, did I no' tell you? He is here alright. And the whole place is swarming with redcoats. Hearken the grouse! They will tell you. But if, as your girlie says, he went up over that rise then he won't go long hungry. He has plenty of loyal, true friends up there.'

Wee Nancy and Lexy were some ten yards away, throwing stones into the burn. Daddy and I were both keeping a constant watchful eye on them, as the burn was quite deep in places, and swift-flowing after a recent rainy spell. At the back of our minds was the warning of the death bird, the mavis, which made us doubly vigilant.

The bairns must have seen the food, but they had been too well tutored to approach and show their hunger. Daddy shouted to them. 'Come here, weans!' The big man was busy spalling the hen and rabbits apart with his hands and laying the pieces on top of the cloths. 'Come on, eat up then,' he said. 'Oh, we are no' hungry, Mister!' wee Lexy cried. 'It's all right, weans,' Daddy said, looking at them with such deep devotion and compassion that I knew I would be forgiven for my recent forbidden behaviour.

I sat the two of them down on the block of a tree and gave them full and plenty to eat. Daddy had refused when I offered some to him, and I had as yet abstained—wondering whether it was right that I should eat when Daddy hadn't— but hunger prevailed. I consoled myself by telling myself that I was not really grown-up yet, as I stuffed delicious curried rabbit into my mouth.

Daddy and the big man were again deep in conversation. So I took the bairns for a wee walk, showing them the rabbit runs, and where I would set a snare. The buds and different kinds of trees I also showed them, and pointed out the rookery, where there were already many nests, and told them how to distinguish rooks from crows. Then I played games with them, leap-frog and tig, but still Daddy showed no sign of going home. So we wandered back to where he and Cameron were still newsing and cracking.

Looking down at the tent I could see that there was no sign of life, and knew that Mother and Katie were not back yet. I knew that Daddy was ettling to get home now, but big Cameron was loath to let him go. 'What time would it be?' Daddy asked him, having noticed a watch chain across his chest. 'Time, man? Time? Who wants to know the time?'

'Well, it's like this, you see,' Father answered him. 'I promised to meet my wife and other lassie, coming back from the town, and you ken what women are if you don't keep a promise.' 'Well, well then, away with you, but don't forget your promise to me either. I will be looking for you and the girlie, mind now and come.' 'I'll try my best,' Daddy said as he started walking away.

We ran and joined Daddy. 'Did ever you see a man like that?' he said. 'He cannae crack.' Then Daddy started laughing. 'What are you laughing at?' I asked. 'Hearken the grouse!' he replied. 'Aye,' I replied, 'and Charlie!' 'I'll bet you he's not poor either,' Daddy continued. 'Did you ever see a man with hair so long in all your life? Were you no' feared of him, lassie?' 'Aye, at first I nearly died.' So we walked down to the tent, discussing Cameron all the way.

'I would like to be picking a fight with him, I ken h(couldn't give you a beating.' (This. is a way of speaking peculiar to travellers. First, they will sometimes say just the opposite of what they mean. And by 'you' they always mean 'anyone'. For instance a traveller will say 'Aye, maybe *you* no' having a smoke all day and him blowing the smoke in *your* face.' This means *any* poor body not having a smoke all day and *anyone* tormenting him by blowing smoke in his face. I doubt if I am capable of making this way of speaking clear to you. It *is* rather difficult to explain!)

25

Anyway, by the time that we reached the tent, I had gathered that Cameron wanted Daddy and me up to his house that night, and had told him to be sure to bring his pipes. He wanted to hear me play too, as he had never heard a girl play. 'Will you watch the weans till I go and see if your mother is coming?' 'Well, give me a match,' I answered, 'and I'll light a fire and put the kettle on. "Hearken the Grouse" wouldn't tell us the time.' And so Cameron was nicknamed 'Hearken the Grouse' from then onwards.

I had just hung the big iron kettle on to the chitties when I heard my parents and Katie approach. Katie was carrying a can of milk and two bunches of hay for the pony. Lexy and Nancy ran to meet them and I heard Mother say 'I ken my weans are no' hungry.' 'Aye, they're starving,' Father answered her. 'Where would you get anything for them here?' she looked at him questioningly. 'I'll tell you after,' he said.

Mother took her big square basket off her arm and, laying it down on the ground, lifted some sweeties out of it.

Then, setting herself down on an upturned dup tin, she turned to the weans and said 'And what has my wee younkers been doing today?'—taking one on either knee as she spoke, and sharing out the wee poke of sweeties. Soon they were telling her of the big hairy giant as she stroked their hair and kissed them.

The pony was tethered near the tent, and Daddy went over with the hay and gave it some. Katie was taking bread, butter, and cheese out of Mother's basket, and I was masking the tea.

After we had eaten, Daddy asked Mother how Willie, Bella and the bairns were keeping, knowing that she would have gone to see them. 'Oh, dinnae speak aboot them,' she said. 'Dinnae mention their names to me. I couldn't believe my eyes when I went in there today. She is nearly at the dropping again—and her baby only eleven months old! Never in all the born days of my life have I heard of such a thing among travellers. They *will* marry blue bucks, you see. Our name will be a speakalation amongst all the other travellers. This is what they get for putting a wean on the bottle.'

Mother was upset and Daddy spent some time trying to get her in good humour again, by telling her about big Cameron and other things. Later he asked if she was sure that she didn't mind us going off to Cameron's house. She assured us that she would be alright as the camp was pretty isolated, and that no one was likely to bother her. So Daddy got his pipes, which were in a wooden box with leather straps on it, and strapped them on his back. Then he put me on the bar of his bike and we set off. But the road was steep and soon we were forced to walk. 'I will push the bike,' he said. 'It will be handy coming back.' Cameron had said 'about three miles' but they must have been Irishman's miles, because as yet we had seen no road to a farm called Pittendriech, and I am sure we had walked at least five miles.

Some distance further on we saw a big house in the distance. 'That can't be it,' Daddy said. 'That is more like a mansion than a farmhouse. We will go up the old road anyway and see.'

There was a pond some two hundred yards from the house, and when I had read a notice board which was stuck on a post beside the pond, I laughed and said 'This *must* be it, Daddy!' The notice read: *Anyone found fishing on the loch, or off the loch or round about the loch shall be prosecuted. First they'll be drowned, then they'll be burned, and then they'll be hung, and, if they come back any more, worse than all of these citations.*

'Aye, this must be Cameron's house,' Daddy said, when I read it to him. 'Nobody else would put up a notice like that,' he said, laughing. More laughter was impossible to suppress, when a little nearer the house we saw a tiny little dog no bigger than a rabbit, occupying an extra large kennel, with a notice up, which read, *Beware of the dog*.

There were several golden pheasants in an enclosure near the house and an aviary ran along one side of the house. I had never seen so many beautiful birds. Wide steps led up to the door, and on the bottom one sat a big crow, which had only one leg. 'Hello,' it said, in a guttural voice, as we approached. Daddy and I exchanged glances. Neither of us had ever heard a crow talk before, although we had had a pet jackdaw which could say a few words. 'Hello! Hello!' it repeated.

26

Someone must have seen us coming. Cameron was standing at the door, and again I was struck by the magnificence of the man.

'I see that you've met Hoppity,' he said. The crow, hearing his voice, did start to hop—and seemed to get airborne without any difficulty, in spite of having only one leg. It landed on Cameron's shoulder. 'No, no, now, not tonight,' the big man said, as he extracted it from his shoulder and gave it a throw in the air. I watched it fly to a nearby tree. 'I have had him since he was a fledgling. He had got caught in netting wire and one of the cats was just about to have him for supper.'

A woman appeared in the doorway. 'Ah, Meeshie, there

you are.' She had very large dark eyes and the eyebrows above them were so highly arched that they gave her the look of being perpetually surprised. In spite of this she immediately gave me the impression of a bird. Her hands and head were always on the move. She fluttered (there is no other word for it) down towards me. 'Come in, come in,' she said, taking my hand, then immediately darted to the other side of me and took my other hand. I could feel some kind of tremor or fluttering going all through her body.

The room we entered was very large and comfortable-looking, with two large sofas and deep armchairs. One of the chairs was occupied by a large brown hen, three cats sat near a black and white border collie on the hearth rug. There was a cradle beside another large armchair near the fire. It had a tiny baby in it.

A girl came through from another room. I knew that she must be a daughter, from the tawny hair and hazel eyes. 'Ah there you are, Isla,' Cameron said. 'You can entertain Betsy while I get her father a drink. Sit down, man.'

I took the girl to be about eighteen. The girl turned to me and smiled. She had a quick smile which lingered on for at least three minutes. She led me to a sofa at the other end of the room.

The mother, who had disappeared, came back into the room with three young women. 'I will introduce you all,' she said. 'This is Kate, Jess and Jean, our three treasures,' she said. The girls were all plump and cheery-looking and spoke with a broad Aberdeenshire accent. 'Treasures indeed,' I thought, as I noted the cleanliness of everything. 'My daughter Isla,' the woman continued, 'and Brownie the hen. Billy the dog and Penny, Penny-Halfpenny, and Penny-Farthing the cats.'

Then, going to the cradle, 'This is young Cameron.' 'Your son?' Father asked. 'Well, yes and no,' Cameron answered. 'I'll tell you about it later.'

He had a bottle of whisky in one hand and two glasses in the other. 'Now before you pour that out, Cameron, I'd better tell you that I'm not a drinking man.' 'Och, you will have a wee dram, surely.' Cameron poured the whisky, ignoring Father's protests. 'I've never met one of *you lads* that couldn't take a dram.' 'Well, you have met one now,' Father said.

I was ignoring Isla's attempts to entertain me, and listening to my father and Cameron instead. I knew that nothing or nobody would persuade Father to drink the whisky, and I wondered about the outcome.

'Come on, man.' Cameron was getting a bit red in the face. 'Sorry, man, I cannot take your whisky.' At this Cameron roared an oath which brought his wife and the servants running in from the kitchen. Poor Father was also changing colours. I knew that should he feel inclined Cameron could lift Daddy up and break his back over one of his knees. Cameron was ranting now. 'A bloody man that cannot take a drink is not fit company even for one of my pigs.' His wife and the girls were trying to pacify him.

I could not bear to see my Daddy in this situation, so I got up and approached Cameron. Walking straight up to him, I shouted 'Don't you dare insult my father like that. I thought you were a gentleman.' He scuddled away from me, a mixture of expressions on his face.

Then he threw back his head, opened his mouth, and laughter gurgled from his throat. Soon they were all laughing, even Daddy. It was then that I realised how funny I must have looked. Me, the skinny little sharger of our family. Yet I felt a bit annoyed at them all laughing at me.

'What a girlie! What a girlie!' Cameron was still shaking with laughter. 'She is right, of course, and I sincerely apologise. But, man, I was so looking forward to a good night's fun.' 'And we will have a good night's fun,' Daddy answered. 'I don't need drink to be funny.' 'Nor does your daughter,' Cameron said, laughing again. 'Come, all of you, into the dining room. Dinner is ready.'

Mrs Cameron shepherded us through the large kitchen and into another room where a large table was set. It was covered with a spotless, white, starched, linen tablecover and real silver ashets and cutlery were all set out, as were beautiful china dishes. Kate and Jess were also asked to sit at the table. 'Tonight it is Jean's turn to serve,' Mrs Cameron said.

Now I had never before sat at a table like this—or at any table for that matter—except, perhaps, having a cup of tea with some cottar or other, and I wondered what in the world one was supposed to do with all those forks, knives and spoons. Father felt much the same although he had used cutlery when in the army and in hospital. 'If you will excuse us,' Daddy said, 'we will just take a wee walk and come back after you have eaten. We have already eaten.'

'You will just sit where you are.' It was Jean who spoke and I just loved her Aberdeenshire tongue. She ladled lovely broth from a silver tureen into plates and set them before us.

Isla started to talk. She had travelled and had been at a school in England and at one in France, and she could make words paint pictures. Apparently her mother, Meeshie, was French, and her real name was Michelle.

Meanwhile I had managed to get through the soup by watching which spoon everyone else used, and Jean had laid out dishes of roast potato, cabbage, carrots, peas, one large leg of roasted pork and one of lamb. Cameron carved these joints and Jean packed plates of food and set them in front of us.

I was at a complete loss with this lot. How could one eat peas holding forks the way they did? It looked so good, too. I wished that I could have sat on the floor and eaten it my own way, with the forks that God had given me. I did try to eat like them, but it was no use. When I tried to cut the meat I sent peas flying all over the lovely tablecover. I felt just terrible. I sent appealing looks to Daddy, but there was no way he could help me.

Isla was still talking and, although I just couldn't properly concentrate on her brilliant use of words, I did gather that Cameron was the son of a Scottish laird and that his Christian name was also Cameron.

Jean was still carrying in more food. 'In the name of God how much are they going to eat?' I thought. A large salmon set on a bed of lettuce and garnished with parsley. It came to the table whole with its head still on and its tail curled up to its mouth. 'Caught him myself yesterday,' Cameron said.

Still more and more food followed. Cheese dishes,

steamed puddings and custard puddings. I had completely lost touch with the conversation, but I could still hear—as if in a distance—Isla's voice and the laughter of the others when she said something particularly witty. My inside was all crined into a knot with embarrassment. At last I saw them get up and murmered a silent 'Thank God' but too soon, too soon.

We were seated back in the living room and brought more food. Coffee, tea, scones, cakes, biscuits. 'Their insides must be like middens,' I thought. Nobody in this world of God's needed so much to eat.

During the partaking of this Daddy talked. 'Cameron,' he said, 'I am going to tell you a wee story, and maybe when you have heard it you will understand why I couldn't take your whisky.' 'Surely, surely, man. Tell us.' 'Well, you see, it was like this,' and Daddy began to tell them about the time he had been held in prison. 'I was as big a drunkard as ever lived,' he told Cameron. 'Drinking every penny I earned, coming home upsetting my wife and bairns and making life miserable for them. Encouraging my wife to drink with me and fighting and tareing with her.'

As Daddy spoke I had vague memories of this. Mother's screams, seeing her with black eyes or the blood pouring from her nose. Daddy in as bad a state, as Mother was a strong determined woman. The morning after, when they would be so ill that they couldn't lift their heads. Their apologies and vows of never again.

'I tell you this, Cameron,' Daddy was saying, 'I went through Hell's torment for four days and nights in that cell—and the worst part of it was not knowing whether I had hit the man or not. I just couldn't remember and, if John Whyte had never regained consciousness, I would have gone to my grave still not knowing. Right enough the bairn did see him falling off the cart, but I didn't know that at the time. Anyway, who would have believed her? I could well have been hanged. So I swore on the blessed Bible that strong drink would never enter my mouth again.'

'Och och, man, I don't blame you.'

By this time the girls had finished clearing and washing the dishes and came to join us.

77

'Jess, it's time this baa-by was fed,' Mrs Cameron said. Jess was a black-haired, rosy-cheeked girl of about twenty or so. She lifted the baby which had slept soundly since our arrival. 'I'll just tak' him ben the kitchie.' 'No, you will not.' Mrs Cameron placed a little wooden nursing chair near the fire and added 'You will just sit there and feed him. I am sure Sandy and Bessie have seen a bairn getting fed before.' The girl sat down, opened her blouse and started to feed the baby.

I looked at the clock and noted that it was an hour and a half since we started eating.

'Come on, and we will hae a wee stroll, Sandy, and I will let you see the place before it gets too dark,' Cameron said to Father. 'Can I come too?' I asked. They both nodded.

Already it was gloaming, and as we passed the aviary I said to Cameron 'These are surely your wife's.' He nodded. 'Yes,' he said, 'she seldom goes away now, and her birds are her hobby.'

The farm was exceptionally large, as was the house itself, and everything was well maintained. 'Come and see my beasts.' Cameron took us first to the byre. 'I just keep twa milk cows for my own use. They will be getting milked soon.' The stable was so cosy with nine large working Clydesdales, two other horses and a riding pony. They had just been fed and freshly bedded and were all munching away at their hay.

A little black and white bundle of mischievous puppy came bounding out of an empty stall, followed by another and yet another. 'Come and meet my Betsy,' Cameron said. 'She has a litter of five and she won't mind you admiring them.' Betsy was a Border collie, like the one we had seen in the house. The puppies were jumping all over us. I sat on my knees cuddling and petting them.

'Would you like one for yourself?' Cameron asked me. 'Oh yes, yes!' I almost shouted. My dog had been killed with a car the summer before. 'Well, take your pick.' 'But these are valuable dogs,' Father said. 'No matter, let the girlie have her choice.'

Just then I noticed one puppy which was not romping

about like the others. It was smaller, the sharger in fact. It was lying with its head on its outstretched paws, looking up into my face with two of the most hypnotic brown eyes I had ever seen. I put my hand out slowly towards it and felt the quiver which ran through its body as I touched it. I looked up at Daddy, saw his slight nod and said 'This one please, Cameron.'

'Look,' he said, 'I told you that you can have any one of them. What about this one?' he said, holding aloft a truly beautifully marked curly-haired one. 'No—this one, please, Cameron.' 'You don't have to take the ugliest one and the sharger at that. Come on, girl, be sensible. Look at this other beauty here.' 'This one, *please*,' I repeated. 'Oh, well, have it your own way.' The puppy no longer recoiled from me, but was licking my fingers without ever taking its brown eyes off my face. 'I'll get him for you before you go.'

There had been lanterns in the stable left there for the maid to take into the byre when she came out to milk the cows. It was almost dark out, so we returned to the house. 'I'll show you around some other day,' Cameron said.

The house was like a little palace. Everything had been tidied. The cats were being put out. The dogs and the brown hen were already out. (Isla told me that Brownie came in every day to lay.) Meeshie was sitting mothering the baby which had been bathed and changed and looked as if he would rather be back in his cradle, being barely able to keep his eyes open.

'Now then, Kate, go and fetch the boys.' Kate went out and returned soon afterwards with four young ploughmen. 'The drinks, Jess.' Cameron treated his servants as equals almost. 'Now then, boys, get seated doon and Jess will give you all a drink.' There was even home-made lemonade for Isla and me, and a dish of oranges and apples. I could have fain slipped outside for a smoke, but I thought better of it.

'First we want to hear the girlie on the pipes.' Daddy took his pipes out of the box and handed them to me. I played *The Highland Wedding*, *The Piper's Bonnet* and *The Mouse among the Barley*. I had been practising those three for weeks. Their applause and praise would have swollen my head tenfold, Cameron's especially. 'My God, man, she really can play. She has good fingers, really good fingers.'

Then Daddy played. He was not an outstanding piper, but was still above average. *Over the Top*, *The Shepherd's Crook*, and *The Sheep Wife*. He too was praised warmly, but Cameron said 'That girlie's going to beat you one day, Sandy.' 'Well that wouldn't be hard to do, Cameron. Her mother's folk are all good pipers.'

One of the young ploughmen could also play the pipes. Another one had a fiddle and one had an accordion. Meanwhile the girls kept dishing out the whisky and bottles of beer. Cameron had already scoffed more than a bottle of Scotch and numerous beers without any apparent effect. Meeshie too had taken a few, as had the girls. Even Isla had one or two. I too wanted to taste it, but Daddy searched for my eye, found it and shook his head.

'What aboot the kye?' Kate had spoken and almost immediately they all burst out laughing. 'Well, they will hae tae be milked,' Kate continued. 'So you want to milk the kye this time, do you, Kate?'

Cameron turned to Father and said, 'We had a ceilidh here aboot ten months ago, Sandy, and I sent Jess and a ploughman lad out to do the milking, and there in the cradle is what she came back in with.' 'Ach, but the twa of them were gey fu',' Jean put in. 'Well anyway, enough is enough. So, Kate, if you want to go and do the milking, none of the lads are going with you. You see, Sandy,' Cameron went on, 'the young lad was getting married in a fortnight's time to a lassie from Meigle. Very fond of her, he was. So he was married and settled before Jess even knew that she was knickit, and there was no use breaking up a marriage. So we never have told him. Anyway it was my fault, sending them out there together and them soused with whisky. So that's why I look upon the infant as mine really. I had always wanted a son and Jess was more than willing to let Meeshie and me adopt him. But, mind, it wasn't done intentionally.'

How good these people were, I thought. No condemning of the young couple. No blaming Jess. Instead he took the blame himself. Still I thought that if I were in Jess's situation I would be more than ashamed of myself. How could she be so brazen and above all how could she give away her baby? This thinking was of course due to the travellers' ways. In those days a traveller girl would be made to suffer dearly if she had a child in these circumstances, and I was very young and stupid at that time.

The party was still swinging. Isla had decided that she would do the milking and I asked if I could accompany her. Kate, Jess, Jean and Meeshie were dancing a Schottische to the music of the accordion. We could hear the hoochs of them as we crossed the dark yard.

When we entered the stable for the lantern I ran to have a look at Ricky, as I had already christened the puppy. He whimpered and edged slowly towards me while the others started romping wildly around me and jumping all over me. Ricky's eyes had found mine again and I spoke softly to him, telling him that I would be coming for him soon.

'Come on, Bessie.' Isla was getting impatient. So I followed her to the byre. I got a milking stool and started to help. I had often helped the maids at farms so I managed not too badly.

Isla talked jokingly about her parents. Cameron had been a disappointment to his father, spoiling all attempts to educate him properly and to make him fit to take over his father's estate. I gathered that he had been rather high-spirited and difficult to bridle. So his father had sort of banished him abroad. He had spent much of his spirits and also much of his father's money, before returning with Meeshie and settling in the glen. They married too late to have more than one child.

'Well, anyway, they made a very good job of that one child,' I said. Isla was visibly pleased. 'Ah, do you really mean that?' she asked. 'I am truly sincere,' I said, and I was. I was astonished really that such a pair could produce a girl like Isla. So well-balanced. So quick-witted. So quick to see things as they really were. 'Sometimes I get a bit depressed and unsure,' Isla said. I knew exactly what she meant and hastened to reassure her, without saying anything wrong about her parents. 'There is more in you than meets the eye, Bessie,' she said, as we carried the milk to the dairy.

As we crossed the yard to go back to the house, I was suddenly aware that someone was playing the pipes, and I *mean* playing. Not Father, not the ploughman, but someone who made a tremor go all through my body and I became hen-skinned all over. 'Isla, who is that playing?' 'Sounds like Father,' she answered, and it was. Huge, clumsy-looking Cameron—fingering the long intricate grace notes of a pibroch with a sensitive yet rattling sound, which would have moved the heart of anyone familiar with pipes.

Daddy was so carried away that he scolded the girls and young men for talking, and propelled Meeshie, who was well on and fluttering all over the place, to a large chair and planted her there, putting his fingers to his lips. 'Sit at peace, goot-bird,' he said to her. 'Shaness, Daddy,' I whispered, trying to suppress laughter. 'I'll be banished,' he said, barely managing to control his own laughter.

I then sat down on the floor at Daddy's knees and we both gave our attention to Cameron. His big drone almost touched the quite high ceiling and his long red hair and bearded face made him look like someone from the last century. (At that time men were almost all clean shaven, and close cropped.) Daddy was saying 'I am shamed to death to have played in front of a man like that.' 'Aye and me too,' I whispered. 'He *cannot* play anyway.' Daddy's answer was a long 'Mmmmm.'

27

After sincerely praising Cameron's piping, we told them that we must get home. So after bidding goodnight to all, and collecting my puppy and a basket of leftovers from the meal (which I had broadly hinted for) we were on our way, with Cameron's voice calling after us—for at least the third time—'Hearken the grouse and let me know if you see Charlie.' As we walked down to where he had left his bike, Daddy said 'He is right enough, you ken. The grouse would let you ken if there was anyone about.' I had the puppy in my bosom above the belt of my coat so that it couldn't fall out, and with the basket in my hand I jumped on to the bar of Daddy's bike and in no time we were near the tent. The rest of the way was over rough moorland and as we approached we could hear that there was someone else there.

It was a policeman and when we came into the light of the fire he said 'Aye aye, and where have you two been at this time of night? Stealing or poaching, I'll bet.'

He then suddenly grabbed me and dragged wee Ricky out of my bosom saying, 'What have you got hidden in there?' He had somehow got the puppy by the tail and it was hanging upside down yelping. Before he could upright it I rushed at him and grabbed it, saying 'You bastard, you are hurting my puppy!' I could hear Katie and Mother's 'Shaness, shaness,' but I wasn't caring. The youngish policeman soon recovered from his surprise and, lifting the basket which I had set down, he also lifted the tea cloth which Isla had covered the food with and was peering into the basket.

At this point Father, who had not spoken a word and who had been standing in the shadows of the fire, stepped forward. His lower jaw was pushed forward as far as it would go, his tongue was sticking out at the corner of his mouth and his eyes rolling upwards.

'That's no' for you, man,' he said. 'That's Prince Charlie's supper. Just you leave it alone or I'll have the policeman from Dooly to you.' He took the basket out of the astonished bobby's hand, and handed it to Mother. 'Poor Charlie has had to go supperless to sleep tonight, but if I had had this with me,' he said, as he pulled the heavy strong snottum out of the ground, 'I would have killed all the redcoats that's in the glen.' He then began brandishing the iron and muttering about Charlie and redcoats in the weirdest voice imaginable. The policeman was visibly disturbed, and Mother said 'Now didn't I tell you that my man was not very weel?'

The bobby, however, was almost out of earshot by the time she had finished speaking, and what with not paying attention to where he was stepping, his feet were soaking. There were a lot of little boggy patches on the moor.

We laughed half the night. 'I can see his face yet,' Katie said. 'God forgive me,' said Father, ' but that is what he deserves.' Mother had whispered to Daddy in cant that the policeman had been leering at Katie for more than an hour. That is why he had put on the exhibition for him. 'He wanted to see the bairns' school attendance cards and said that we must be out of here tomorrow,' Mother continued. 'He has been here since nine o'clock.' 'I suppose they will be up wi' a straitjacket for me in the morning!' Daddy was laughing as he said it.

'What do you think we should do, Maggie?' Daddy was beginning to sober up as it were. 'If Peesie hadn't ran away from school there would have been none of this carry-on!' Katie shouted. (Peesie was her nickname for me, because every springtime I would go collecting peewits' eggs.) 'Dinnae Peesie me!' I shouted back at her. 'You always eat your share of the peesies eggs.' Katie and I always seemed to rub each other the wrong way.

'You're beginning to come out of your buckie, wee woman.' Mother said to me. 'That was a way to curse in front of a policeman.' 'I am awfully worried about him with the horse's jaws,' I answered her. 'That's enough out of you, get into bed. You too, Katie, till I get peace to think what we're going to do,' said Father. 'And you're not taking that animal in beside the weans.'

Poor wee Ricky. I could feel him quivering where I had replaced him in my bosom. 'The wee creature is frightened to death.' I took him out gently and talked to him. 'Dinnae be feared, cratur, poor wee darling, and you just ta'en awa' fae yer mammie.' I cuddled him and crooned to him until his little body stopped shaking. Then I warmed some milk for him and gave him a wee bit of the meat from the basket. Then, putting him into an old carton with an old jersey under him, I placed him at the back of the tent near my feet.

The pony was yoked when I got up after being wakened by Mother. All the rest of them were already up and wee Lexy was sitting near the fire cuddling Ricky. He looked up and started to wag his tail when his eyes met mine, but I only had time to give him a wee pat and say good morning to him, as there was the tent to take down and all the tidying up to do.

'God pity that policeman, him with the long face. No wonder you called him Horse's Jaws.' Mother was not in a very good mood that morning. She probably hadn't had any sleep all night.

We had to carry everything quite a bit to where the yoke was on the road, but soon all was ready and we hit the road. I was ordered to get inside the cart to look after little Lexy and Nancy, lest they should fall out. Katie and Mother walked. 'Where are we going?' I asked Father. 'Not very far,' he answered. 'I'll mebbe just go up to the Den of Alyth and put youse to school from there. We were home early last year and youse only need about thirty more attendances.' 'That's fifteen days,' I said. 'Aye, three weeks. If that policeman doesn't shift us again.'

But we were not to get to the Den of Alyth—for who should we meet on the road but Cameron, although it was no more than seven o'clock. 'What's this, then, what's this?' he said as Father pulled up to talk to him. 'Would you be for going off without saying eechie or oichie?' 'I have to shift, man,' Father told him. 'The police was up last night.' 'Oh, was he, now, was he?' Cameron had taken hold of the pony's bridle and, without saying more, turned the yoke round on the road. Then he started leading the pony back the way we had come.

Soon we met Mother and Katie. 'What are you doing now?' Mother shouted to Father, eyeing big Cameron with wary eyes. Although we had told her about him I don't think she was quite prepared for the enormity and strange appearance of this bearded giant. 'You are all coming back with me,' Cameron told her. 'You must be the good woman herself are you? Up you get beside your man then,' and to Katie, 'you too, girlie.' He led the pony all the way.

'I was just on my way to see you,' he continued. 'I was out shooting and I have two fine hares in my bag for you.' 'It is very good of you,' Mother said, 'but we don't eat hares. Rabbits, but not hares.' 'Och well, but I have rabbits too.'

Just then some startled pheasants rose over on the moor

a bit. 'Hearken, hearken the grouse. Those bloody redcoats are everywhere. One of these days I'll find the bonny laddie and get him out of their reaches. I'll mak' mincemeat of the redcoats.' Mother nor Father didn't bother to answer him. I think they were too weary.

The bairns started to laugh, but I shushed them, and asked Cameron who had taught him to play the pipes. He instantly forgot Charlie and told us about a wonderful old gamekeeper who had been on his father's estate, and who had taught him the bagpipes. He talked of his father, of India and New Zealand and other foreign countries, until we came to his farm.

'Now, anywhere you want to stay, just pitch your tent. No policeman will shift you from here.' 'That's a' right, and right enough, Mr Cameron, but it's a awfu' long way for to walk from here to Alyth, and I have to look for a living for my bairns.' Mother was not too happy about being so far up the glen. 'It's more than good of you to give us a place to live, but I doubt we can't stay long.'

'Have you any work for us to do?' Father asked. 'Work? Aye, plenty work. The fields are all drilled for the potatoes and the turnips were sowed last week so there's work enough. I usually get a squad up from the village but if you can do them, well, so much the better.'

Mother chose a nice spot for our tent, about a quarter-mile from the farm and near running water. Katie gathered sticks, I got water, Father put up the tent and soon the tea was ready. The bairns were playing with Ricky. I was hurrying to get finished so that I too could get playing with him. He had not whimpered all the previous night, though Mother had expected him to.

Cameron needed more people for his potato planting, so Father went into Blairgowrie on his bike the following day, and persuaded his brother Willie to come up the glen. Willie had five grown-up sons and six daughters. The boys or men would not plant the potatoes. They considered that women's and children's work, but they would load and carry for them. Cameron and his wife were more than generous: potatoes, milk, eggs, and sometimes a bit of fresh butter and cheese. He also told the vanman, who came twice a week, to give us anything that we wanted. He would keep the money off our pay.

We had found a little haven and—but for the sorrow when one of Mother's nieces died in childbed—this would have been the happiest, most pleasant, springtime in our lives. I was not very much acquainted with my cousin Bella who had died but, when Daddy and Mother were unhappy, we were unhappy too.

28

Travellers don't try to keep control of themselves in grief. They just let it rip through them.

Women and men crying like babies, refusing food for days, just drinking tea and smoking—and stupefying themselves with whisky, although this practice has almost died out now. Most of us are determined that our children should not be subjected to this, the most frightening of all experiences for a child: seeing a parent—or worse still, both parents—stupidly drunk. I believe that this can have detrimental effects on young children. I have vague memories of my own childhood before Daddy stopped drinking. They seemed like people from another world, a world of completely mad people, and I was terrified— fearing that they would remain like that and never regain their sanity. Not that they were ever cruel or unkind in drink: the opposite, in fact. We were showered with anything that they could possibly afford to get us, but what we really wanted was our Mammie and Daddy back from that alien world.

Bella was buried in Logierait, the child with her, and Daddy had stayed somewhere up there for three days, allowing Mother to drink most of this time with her sorrowing relatives. Of course all the men from our camp were away up to the funeral too. Travellers then, and to this day, will gather from all directions and go for many miles to a funeral, offering to help in any way possible. Katie was left in charge of us, and Uncle Willie's youngest son and oldest daughter were left to look after things and keep Katie company: the women also going to the funeral.

I can remember so well the first night that they went away, because on that night I had the pleasure of seeing a truly wonderful sight. I was sitting beside an outside fire in the gloaming when I noticed strange flashes in the sky, right away out over the hills. At first I thought that it was lightning, and gathered in the washing and any shoes and things that were outside, putting them safely under canvas. Resuming my seat, I waited for the claps of thunder and watched the strange lights in the sky. No thunder came, but the flashes continued. Then I noticed that they did not come from one direction. They were all around, and varying in shape and colour—and beautiful. Mother told me when she returned that it must have been wildfire, whatever that is.

The woman who had died was no more than thirty. Her husband, who was the son of my father's brother, came back with them. His name was Hendry, and my father was very fond of him. He was a pitiful-looking creature, absolutely distraught and continually blaming himself for his wife's death because she had died in childbed. He didn't stay long with us, but chased himself here and there, from one encampment to another, continually drinking and rarely eating. Wherever he went people would give him money for his drink, knowing that whisky had great healing powers—although knowing also that his drinking bout was taking much too long, and everyone was worried about him.

Mother, on the other hand, was quick to patch up the rent made on her spirit by Bella's death and was soon her normal self again, as was Father. Father didn't work at the potato-planting, but he worked when the turnip-thinning time came. We stayed up there till the end of May.

Cameron was a frequent visitor, often bringing rabbits and trout to us. He never bothered us at work at all. In fact he left all the running of the farm to a very competent young grieve, to his foreman and other ploughmen; and a very good job they made of it. Cameron preferred to ramble through the glen doing whatever he felt like doing.

On Sundays we never worked, not even women's work,

except what was absolutely necessary. Sunday's food was all prepared on the Saturday nights. Children were bathed early, then the grown-ups cleaned themselves up too for Sunday coming. Although they never worked on Sundays, they certainly played.

There was a grass park at the back of Cameron's house. They erected goal posts in it and Cameron and the ploughmen and the men from the camp played football, cricket, rounders and other games. Sometimes they played quoits or pitch and toss. No girls or women were allowed to participate, but we had great fun just watching. Cameron's antics and reactions were hilarious. He was clearly enjoying himself and didn't mind our laughter one bit.

Sometimes they would go hunting hares. Uncle Willie had two greyhounds and Cameron had his dogs too. The men even accompanied him one time on his search for Prince Charlie, but this occasion nearly brought a tragedy. One of Willie's boys borrowed a red blazer from one of the women and, putting it on, he ran ahead and bobbed up in front of them. Of course he ran ahead by a different route so that Cameron didn't see him go, but nearly cost him his life.

Without hesitation Cameron had let fly with his shotgun, shouting 'Down with the bloody redcoats!' Luckily for the boy he was at some distance and escaped with only two pellets in one of his legs. This incident sobered the men up a bit, there was no more Charlie-hunting and when Cameron brought up the subject they quickly diverted him. But they never did tell him that he had hit the boy.

Often, too, as the nights lengthened, they had wonderful ceilidhs in which the girls and women were welcomed. Daddy had acquired a melodeon from one of the ploughmen and one of Uncle Willie's boys played a fiddle. Sometimes I played the pipes, and Isla turned out to be a very proficient Highland dancer. The men brought a board from the farm for her to dance on. There was singing and story-telling as well.

Isla and I often went walking and talking, after work, with Ricky—who was turning out even more intelligent than I had expected. Although he was friendly with all the family, he was a one-person dog and showed it in many ways. Of course I was that one person. Whoever said that dogs only understand by the tone of your voice was wrong. With his head on top of his outstretched paws, Ricky would look up at me when I started to go anywhere. If I shook my head he would lower his eyes and put his paws up over them, but if I nodded he would jump up, tail wagging, and follow me—without ever a word being spoken. He was so quick to understand what was expected of him.

He used to chase the poultry when I took him with me up to the farm for milk. I don't know if it was my rebukes, or a nasty peck—very near an eye—from Hoppity, or his rather humiliating encounter with a gander, which cured him of that.

He was not the only one who was humiliated by the gander. After rescuing Ricky I was forced to climb up on to the roof of a shed, throwing Ricky up before me. I had to sit up there till one of the maids noticed me, and shooed the gander into an enclosure. My can of milk was spilled, too, and I didn't take the laughter of all the household in very good part. Jean in particular seemed to think that I was very stupid and, as she bandaged a rather nasty gash on my leg, the tears were running down her face with the power of laughter. I don't know whether I had gashed my leg scrambling up the shed, or whether the gander had done it, but I felt very annoyed with Jean for making a fool of me. 'It's no' a' that funny,' I said. 'You shouldn't crow so much. You will maybe do something just as silly before very long.' 'Weel-awyte, I dinnae think so,' she answered.

However, she was wrong. For the very next day she went down to a henhouse which was situated in a field about a hundred yards from the farm. She had gone to feed the hens and collect the eggs. Now there was a billy goat in this field, which had never before paid any attention to her—but this day, head down and horns at the ready, it attacked her. She was forced to lock herself i . the henhouse and spent several hours there before she was found. I would be lying if I said that I didn't gloat a bit when I heard of this. I was still very young.

The next time I saw Jean she said to me, during the conversation, 'I think there is a bit of a witch in you.' I

My photographs

Most people have many photographs of their parents and from their own young days. I have only these seven.

Yet it is still surprising that they have survived. As I explain in my story, we travellers carried only essential and treasured possessions with us. Everything else was burned when we moved on. So most of these photographs must have been among my mother's treasures. She kept them carefully in a little wooden box along with other precious papers such as birth certificates and references from farmers.

My mother and her brothers

In my mother's young days, to have a photograph taken was a nine days' wonder for travellers. Most of them were flattered and eager to comply when asked to pose by a photographer looking for an unusual postcard.

This postcard is entitled 'Aberfeldy tinkers'. This group of 'tinkers' includes my mother — on the right. Next to her, playing the pipes, is her younger brother Jimmie, with her brother Hendry and his wife and child.

The caption on the postcard describes 'tinkers' as 'light-fingered' and 'a race apart, as idle and attractive generally as the gipsy tribes. . . .' This was the feeling of many people when I was young, and it persists today.

Mother and father

Of course it was unusual for travellers to have a photograph taken in a photographer's studio. This one of my parents was taken when Father was home on leave during the First World War — for in wartime even travellers wanted a photograph of their loved ones, lest the worst should happen. It is the only photograph I have of my father, taken before I was born.

But it is a fake. Originally it was a family portrait which had become faded and worn. After Mother died, I cut off the part showing the family and asked a photographer to put Mother and Father together.

This is the only part left of the original family group. It shows my sister Katie and my brother Andy who died soon after this photograph was taken. They are holding the hands of an older sister.

My Family

This is another photograph which was sold as a postcard. It was sent to me recently by a cousin, whose mother had kept it.

It shows my mother on the left and my oldest sister Bella on the right. In front is my brother and the babe in arms is me.

At school

Me, taken by a visiting photographer at school, before the time my story begins in 1930.

This one, too, came from my cousin when I was asking my family and friends if they had any photographs to illustrate my story. I had forgotten that this one existed.

My sister Bella

My sister Bella with one of her three children. I am not sure if this is Donald, who died after a countrywoman 'put her eye' on him, but it may be.

My cousins

Cousins of mine with a 'yoke' of the kind used only by women and children. It was smaller than the men's 'yokes' and was drawn by a 'Shelty' (a Shetland pony) or a 'cuddy' (a donkey).

(Sometimes some of the gentry or visiting foreigners would photograph travellers and return in a few days' time with a copy for them. This is how this photograph was obtained.)

laughed, but her words set me to thinking of the numerous other times when things like this had happened. It was a rather sobering thought to my maturing mind, but I dismissed it. 'You stupid lassie,' I told myself, 'only God can make anything happen. It is a sin even to think like that.'

Then I thought about the peculiar conversations which Daddy and Mammie had been having with me lately, at odd moments. The gist of these conversations was that everybody in the world was good. 'You should never hate another human being. Poor souls, if you only knew what suffering or what frustration was in their hearts, you would not hate them.' 'You should never let anything that people say get under your skin. A word is just a word; it's no' a stick or a stone that can hurt you.' 'Insults are just like a dose of salts. If you don't take them they cannae work,'—and so on. At the time I hadn't paid much attention to these conversations, but now I was trying to recall more of them. Then I recalled those rather peculiar looks which I had caught Daddy giving me lately, and the long deep sighs which he was given to. He had always had this habit of sighing deeply but now they were more frequent.

I sat down on a bank, confused and a bit troubled. It was funny how those few words of Jean's had started what now was a pyramid of thoughts in my head. I sat there, trying to unravel the confusion, but I soon realised that my brain was incapable of doing it at that time. My spirit was too troubled. I looked around for something to soothe it. I looked at the cows and sheep grazing. I looked at the trees budding, especially a willow which was very pretty. I looked at one of the ploughmen who was ploughing a field. His horses had stopped, and he was whistling a peculiar whistle which ploughmen used to help their horses pass their water.

Yes, I did feel less disturbed, so I got up and breathed in deeply the wonderful country air, and shouted to Ricky who was half-way inside a rabbit hole and covered with earth.

29

'What kept you so lang wi' the milk?' Mother asked when I got back to the camp. 'Naething,' I answered her.

'Well, your sister Bella had a wee laddie this morning. Willie is here. I want you to get yourself ready and go down with him to look after the bairns.' 'Me?' I asked. 'What about Katie?' 'Aye, you,' Mother answered. 'Katie says she's no' gaen and, anyway, it's about time that ye learned something about these things.' 'Silly young woman, imagine having a wean and the other one still on hippens. I don't know what the world is coming to.' Mother was nattering away to herself now. I looked at Daddy. 'It will no' be for lang,' he said. 'Your Mother and me will be doon the morn, to see her and to see how you're getting on. It's too late the night now, for us to come doon wi' ye.'

'Then how am I going to get doon?' I asked. 'Willie will tak' you doon on his bike.' 'Aye aye,' I said—and the two words were long and slowly drawn out—'if you wait long enough I'm gan doon a' they braes on the front o' Willie's bike. Sorry, Daddy, no—even if the Pope o' Rome were to ask me. They will surely no' dee for one night. I'll go doon wi' you the morn.' Daddy laughed. 'Shaness, lassie, what will the fella think?' 'I'm no' heedin' what he thinks. How many times has he had accidents wi' naebody but himsel' on the bike? What like would he be wi' twa? Na, na. Sorry, Daddy, I just cannae dae it.'

Just then Willie came in-about. He had been up seeing my Uncle Willie and his family. He grabbed me and pinioned my arms while he rubbed his twenty-four-hour stubble against my cheek. 'Are ye coming wi' me, sister, to see this wee new doll that we have got?' 'I'll be doon the morn,' I told him. 'What's a-dae? Have you gotten yourself a lad up here?' 'No,' I answered him, whilst punching him jokingly, 'but there's nae use me saying one thing and thinking another. I just wouldn't tak' a' broad Europe to sit on your bike gan doon.' Father was affronted at me. 'Lassie, lassie!' he said. 'It's a'right, Sandy,' Willie said. 'I ken her o' auld and I would rather hae her that way.'

Willie was one of my favourite persons. He was not tall nor very good-looking. His nose was much too big. So much so that Bella often called him Ebenezer. He was full of fun and very kind-hearted. 'Can I take Ricky wi' me?' I asked him. 'Please yoursel', but you will have to keep him inside all the time except when you take him out on a lead.' 'I don't think he would like that.' I stood and swithered for a moment then said 'You are right. He would be better here.'

'We'll rise early in the morning and will be doon before dinner time,' my father told Willie as he prepared to go. So next day Daddy yoked the pony, and took Mother and me down to Alyth. I left Ricky lying with his paws over his eyes—keeking out now and then to see if I would change my mind.

Bella looked more beautiful than ever, lying there with her hair down and the light of motherhood in her eyes. Surely motherhood must be the most blissful of all the emotions, I thought, when it can give such beauty to a woman. Mother and Father left in the early evening, after making much of all the children. 'Now, sister, all I want you to do is to watch the weans and mak' a wee bite for them and Bella. Just leave everything else, and I will do it myself when I come home.' Willie was going out on his bike, selling boot and furniture polish, and when he came home the next day about four o'clock, he said 'Wait till you see what I've got for you, sister.'

After he had eaten some of the stew which I had made he went outside and came back in with a box full of the loveliest girl's clothes that I had ever seen—all my size. My eyes nearly goggled out of my head. I loved pretty clothes. 'I asked them, especially for you, from a lady who owns a big house in Rosemount.' A real traveller man would never beg woman's clothes, but Willie would. He was more than good to me, praising my cooking and the way that I was looking after the bairns, with never a word of criticism. True, his ways were different, but before I left there I was beginning to think that his ways were the best. Bella and he were so cheery and happy together. They would lie singing together in bed at night.

I was with them for a month. My parents had shifted to

a camp near Newtyle. Of course they had been in to see us a number of times. During these visits Bella left me to do all the cooking and serving, but whenever they left she was back doing them herself. 'How can a woman be any dirtier just after having a baby than she is at any other time?' she would say. Willie agreed, and eventually I did too. 'For God's sake, don't tell Mammie and Daddy!' she told me. (Travellers always say mammie and daddy, when talking among themselves, even when they are middle-aged.)

30

About this time (the 1930s) the authorities were beginning to close down all the camping grounds and travellers were being stupidly hunted from place to place. I say 'stupidly' because it really was a stupid carry-on. Round about Brechin alone there were five old byways which many travellers had wintered on, schooling their children. One at Trinity, one which we travellers called Powsoddies, one on the Forfar road called The Boat Camp, another one called The Green Tree Old Road, and one at Lightning Hill. All of these camps were within a day's travelling of each other and all had been public highways at one time. So they really belonged to the public and travellers were not trespassing when they lived on them. They had as much claim to these old roads as anyone else.

A policeman or perhaps two would come to Trinity Old Road, and tell them that they would have to move on the next day. So they would shift to the Green Tree, perhaps, and live there a few days before being told to move on again. Then they might go to Lightning Hill. This went on the whole time, and in spite of having to take their tents down in freezing weather and go on for five or six miles, the travellers found this highly amusing. Well, some of them did. They would perhaps meet friends on the road, who had just been shifted off the place that they were going to, and who were going to the place that the others had been asked to leave. Yet somehow or other they managed to let their children get the two hundred school attendances required by law. It was like this all over the country. I am just giving Brechin as an example.

Many farmers were quite agreeable to allowing us to live on their land, provided that we helped with the many jobs which were at that time needing done on the farm. Travellers were very thankful to these farmers, made sure that they did their work well, and would not even take a turnip out of a field without permission. Honesty was essential and any traveller who broke this code was not allowed to stay on the encampment. Other travellers would not live beside them. So most of them lived by this code, lest they should be made outcasts, and have to live by themselves in some isolated place, perhaps. This would have been almost unbearable as, apart from being very lonely, there was always the danger of being attacked by blaggards. Sometimes even the young ploughmen would take it into their heads to have what they called 'a tare' with travellers, when there were just one or two tents. They could sometimes be quite cruel. So honesty was the order of the day.

Daddy much preferred to live on a farmer's ground. That is why he was at Newtyle. It was at a flower farm where they grew daffodils and tulips, and needed people to clean up the fields, and to weed carrots and other vegetables. Living on these farms saved us from being driven about by the police, and also provided a few shillings, so we didn't have to bother people by going round the doors.

31

I was very pleasantly surprised to find several of my aunts and uncles and families were there too: including Uncle Jimmie and Edna. It was so nice to see Annie again. Mary and Johnnie, too, were there and now had a lovely little baby daughter.

During our stay there I accidentally learned that the girl who had been killed by a car was the one who had been so nasty to me at school. Mother and Father had hoped that I would never find this out. I was quite upset. 'Daddy,' I asked, 'do you think that I am like Mother?' 'There is a good bit o' your mother in you, but I have been thinking a lot about it, and I have come up with the simplest possible answer to your problem.'

'Tell me, Daddy.' 'Well, I have been trying to tell you, and so has your mother. If you practise now when you are young. You must never hate anyone or wish anyone ill, nor do anything to harm anyone, even if they deserve it. That way your conscience is clear, and whatever happens you won't feel bad. With a clear conscience you have nothing in the world to fear.' 'Oh, Daddy, you are as bad as yon priest that asked me to swear that I would never sin again.' (This had actually happened.) 'No, no, lassie, listen. This is different a'thegither. It will be hard, I ken, but promise me you will really try your best. You can do no more than that.' 'I'll try,' I answered, 'but ye ken me.'

'You're alright,' he said, and somehow those two words made me very happy. 'You're alright': two plain simple little words, but I cherished them.

My first day back from my sister Bella's had been an unforgettable day for me. Little Lexy and Nancy ran to meet me with Ricky at their heels. So much cuddling, kissing, and licking, and their genuine delight, was food for my soul.

Shortly afterwards Mother said 'I've got something for you. It's from Isla.' Isla! I had thought about her often and wished that I could have seen her before I left and wished her goodbye. Mother came out of the tent and said, 'Hold out your hand and shut your eyes.' I did, and quickly opened my eyes again when I felt something drop on my palm. It was a chain bracelet, real gold with a little padlock and safety chain. I felt a tremor of sheer delight go through my body, and I became all henny-skinned with the depth of it. Isla!

I closed my eyes and remembered our last conversation, as we walked together up the glen. 'Bessie,' she had said, 'do you know that I can talk to you about things, better than I ever could to anyone else, in spite of you being so young and everything? And there is something more I would like to talk about.' 'Isla, I know exactly what you would like to talk about. Will I tell you?' She laughed and said 'Yes, tell me.'

'Well,' I said, 'you would like to talk to someone about your parents. Deep in your heart you feel ashamed because they are, shall we say, a bit eccentric. I don't think that you have ever asked any of your friends up to your house, nor that young man that you are so fond of.' 'Oh, Bessie!' Her face was like a fire. 'How can you possibly know about Cyril? I have never told a living soul.' 'Don't ask me how I know. I don't know that myself, but I do know that you are unhappy about it all.'

'Why should you be, Isla? Your father and mother are two of the most wonderful people that I have ever met, in spite of their little mental quirks—or perhaps because of them. I am sure that your friends would love them and really enjoy visiting you. And any one of them that didn't would have to suffer from a really big mental quirk themselves, the wrong kind.' 'But, Bessie, you should see Cyril's parents! They are so different. He lives in St Andrews and his father is a barrister, so clever and dresses so well, and his mother has house-parties and things. She is so sophisticated.' 'And ordinary, and boring,' I interrupted her. 'Ask Cyril and all your friends up, Isla, and tell them all that you are more than proud of your parents, and you really should be.'

I hoped that Isla would be there when we went back up the glen the following spring. Daddy had promised Cameron that they would be back. Annie was my constant companion there. We did almost everything together. She had grown taller, and was still lovely.

Hendry, the one who had lost his wife, came in-about one day. He looked so awful that I was almost angry with him. That evening, as Annie and I and our mothers were out gathering firewood, I talked about him. Mother and Edna too talked about him.

'Ma, how does he punish himself like that, going about like a sheep from the shears, and not eating?' 'Well, you see, he wants to punish himself. Do you mind when you threw yourself on top of a whin bush and even managed to fall asleep on top of it? Look! There's a whin over there. Let me see you doing that now. Go on!'

'What has that got to dae wi' it?' I asked as I approached the whin. 'Aha, you see,' Mother said, as I 'ouched' and jumped back when only one whin spike came against my bare arm. 'Well,' Mother said, 'you were so sair hurt inside that you were trying to cure it by hurting yourself outside.' 'I wasnae, I never even thought about that.' 'Then how did you lie on a whin bush? Poor Hendry is doing much the same thing, but he thinks that he deserves to be punished.'

'Oh Ma, that is a silly way to think. He didn't kill her. Other men don't think like that. Could it really be because he rues the times that he was a bit hard on her?' 'I suppose there is that an' a' but he was nae waur than other men are to their wives!'

32

Poor Hendry! He looked for punishment and he got more than he bargained for.

One night he failed to come home and around midnight Mother said to Daddy 'I think you should rise and go and look for Hendry. Mebbe your brother Jimmie will go with you.' Father was a bit annoyed. 'I am beginning to get sick of Hendry and his carry-on. He has more than likely went over to where Jean and Johnnie and them are staying near Coupar Angus.'

But Mother was uneasy. 'It will not kill you to go and see if you can see him.' I fell asleep shortly after Daddy went out, but was awakened in the small hours of the morning by voices raised in anger. Mother was saying 'My God, my God, what happened to him?'

Katie and I hurriedly threw something on and jumped out of bed. I pokered up the fire in the dup tin and refuelled it while Katie lit the paraffin lamp.

Uncle Jimmie and Daddy had oxtered Hendry home

from where they had found him, near the village. He had been lying on the grass at the side of the road, badly beaten up. Mother was crying 'My God, laddie, when are you going to stop worrying folk like this? If you are not caring about yourself, surely you should care about the torture you are causing us all to have, worrying about you.' 'Leave him abee, Maggie, he is in a bad way.'

By this time the two men had got Hendry into bed. He was trembling like a leaf. 'Bessie, go and look for a puttin' stane and heat it.' It was still dark and I found a putting stone more from feel than sight. I had remembered where I had seen one and groped around till I felt it. Any other type of stone would crack and break with the heat. I put it on top of the lid of the dup tin to heat.

Daddy was ranting, something he seldom did. 'The double adulterous bull-bitch's son, I'll mak' him in hawk's meat if it's the last thing I ever do. I'll gladly go to the gallows for him.' And so on. I could never remember ever seeing Daddy so angry. Sparks of fury seemed to fly from his eyes and venom-filled blood had rushed to his head, dusking his usually fresh complexion. Even in the light of an oil lamp, or perhaps because of it, he looked so unlike my Daddy that I was frightened.

Daddy was too soft-hearted, however, to examine Hendry himself. Even if any of us children ever cut ourselves, he couldn't dress it. He always shouted for Mother to do it.

But she was upset too. 'Ach ach, anee, Sandy. The poor dear cratur. I'm sure some of his ribs are broken too. He was not suffering enough.' Hendry was muttering 'Dinnae be upsetting yourselves aboot me. I'm sorry, Auntie Maggie, I'm sorry, Uncle Sandy. I'll be alright.' He was obviously in severe pain and still shaking all over. Katie had given Mother a basin of warm water to bathe Hendry's face, also the pot stone wrapped into a piece of blanket to put in the bed at his feet. Soon Mother had his ribs tightly bound with a strip of old blanket, and his face cleaned of the blood with which it had been caked.

I had missed hearing who had beaten him, when I had been out looking for the stone, but I didn't dare to ask at that time. 'There is nae blood coming up your throat, is there?' Mother asked as she held a cup of tea to Hendry's lips. 'No, Auntie, it's just awfully sair when I breathe. Dinnae fash yourself, that blood is coming from my mouth where he knocked out my teeth.'

'The dirty soulless-hearted whore's son!' Daddy was still boiling and tears were in Uncle Jimmie's eyes. 'Man, but he was clever, eh? Battering and kicking a poor cratur who was so drunk that he couldn't lift a hand to save himself. Well done if a black judgment should alight on him. If I had him here right now I would mak' him that he would never chew cheese again.'

'Wheesht, man,' Mother said, handing Father a bowl of tea, 'let him get some rest.' Uncle Jimmie left after drinking his tea.

'You two lassies had better go to bed. You will have to go to your work tomorrow, the farmer is depending on you. They carrots are badly needing thinned out.' Katie and I slept together, for Father had erected a little sleeping place for us. It was added on to the side of the gailie, something like the way that a room is added to a house.

'Who done it?' I whispered to Katie, after we were in bed. 'A toby,' she whispered back, 'one of the ones who were in-aboot here on Saturday.' 'I'll bet it was that one with the bullock eyes,' I said. 'I didn't like the look of him at all.' Three policemen had been going round all the camping sites, looking for someone named Alec McIntosh but they had had a car and we thought they came from Perth.

Next morning Hendry was really ill. Pneumonia, Mother was sure, had set in. 'I'll have to get a doctor to see you, Hendry.' 'No, no, Auntie Maggie, nae doctors. They will put me in the poor's house. Please, Auntie Maggie, if I'm gan tae dee let me dee here.' He spoke with difficulty, and clung to Mother's hand, pleading with her not to get a doctor.

Mother had a difficult decision to make. He was so upset at the thought of hospitalisation that Mother feared it would finish him. Yet she knew that if he died here she would get into trouble for not getting medical attention for him. Already she had poulticed him back and front with mustard. Now she was endeavouring to fill his tent with steam from the spout of a huge iron kettle.

During the next two or three days he was delirious, moaning and heaving his chest. The whole encampment was quiet and subdued. Even Ricky seemed to guess that something was wrong and stayed away from the tent. Father and Mother took an hour or two's sleep in turns. Nancy and Lexy were being looked after by Edna. 'He will tak' the turn tonight about midnight,' Mother said. 'If he gets over that he should be alright.' She was wetting his lips with a feather. 'It was the shock of that beating that brought on the pneumonia, but I think I just may have caught it in time. Poor soul, he must be sair with all they mustard poultices on top of cracked ribs.'

Mother would have made a good nurse. She had some sort of inborn instinct which I have seldom seen in anyone else.

She also had quite a few remedies of her own, but I can remember only a few of them. There is a tiny little yellow flower which has large roots. I never did discover its name, but can remember seeing her prepare the roots when anyone had dysentery or anything similar. She used to roast an onion in the embers, then squeeze out the juice into a cup or something. It was just like an oil of some sort. This she used for earache or a running ear, and never have I seen it fail. Carbolic soap and sugar were creamed together into an ointment which would quickly draw out the root of a boil or lift the scar off a graze which had started to heal.

If anyone got a splinter deep down under a finger or toe nail, she would soak a bandage with castor oil and, making sure it was kept well soaked, leave it on for two or three days. This would draw out the splinter. For gumboils she used a fig and this usually drew it out in a few hours. A pinch of salt in a little milk was used for the eyes. Salt was also used as a gargle for sore throats. Honeycomb, as well as honey, was eaten to clear the chest tubes. Sometimes for adults a whole egg, shell too, was switched into brandy and used for the chest. It was swallowed, crushed shell as well.

Of course these and many other remedies which Mother used were not so good as our modern medicines, but they did help a lot in those days.

Hendry recovered slowly and confirmed that it had been the village policeman who had beaten him up. 'I would have thought nothing of it had I given him provocation, but I was just lying on the bank at the side of the road.' 'The mad brute!' Father said. 'He is mad,' said Mother, 'and I can tell you the reason that he battered you, Hendry, because he seen in you what he himself is coming to. You mark my words. He is never sober as it is.'

We worked there until July. The grown-ups didn't, only the young people and children. When we were not working, Annie and I had some wonderful walks together, and talks. Often we would spend hours sitting high up on a branch of a huge beech tree, other times we would lie in a hayrick reading—usually fairy tales which our mothers brought back from the village.

There were some marshy places around, and one day we spent hours watching the antics of frogs. Hundreds of them were on the march, each with a tiny baby on its back, and the babies didn't fall off even when the big frog jumped. I wondered about these frogs. How in the world could they tell their own babies? There were millions of tiny frogs and half-frogs, half-tadpoles—also newts. Did they just take any baby? I wondered. To this day, I am still none the wiser.

33

Father decided to go to the flax that year instead of the berry-picking.

Few travellers really liked the way we had to live at the berry-picking, so near to the many hundreds of town dwellers that came from far and near to pick the berries. We did not feel completely at ease with so many of them around. Sometimes they would start strikes and marches from one berry farm to another, getting all the other berry-pickers to strike as well. During these strikes they sometimes played havoc with the farmers' property: burning fencing posts and even hayricks and cutting the telephone wires, lest the farmer should phone the police. We wanted no part of this, but we were forced to stay away from work under threat until they had come to some agreement.

On the other hand, if we went to a farm which employed only travellers there was just as much unease.

All travellers have nicknames or, rather, I should say that every different breed of travellers has a different nickname. Our nicknames were beetles, rowans, sugar, roundheads, meals, pigs' lugs, and dannies. All of these breeds were intermarried somehow. Then there were hundreds of other strange nicknames such as brouchans, squirrels, linties, cold kails, kippers, eye of the herrings, and so on.

In those days we were very touchy about nicknames. Children would often innocently mention someone's nickname and start an unholy row. If two or three different breeds were working for one farmer each breed would stay at least a few hundred yards away from each other. Apart from this thing about nicknames, different travellers had different ways and didn't like even other travellers to be too familiar. Their basic way of life and superstitions were all the same, but each breed had its own peculiarities.

So we went to the Bridge of Earn for the flax, about five families of us—mostly my father's brothers and their wives. The flax was still in flower when we arrived at the farm: a beautiful sea of blue with the glaggen's silvery waves almost blinding me as I gazed across the field. What caused this glaggen? I wondered. Could it possibly be the webs or silken threads of the millions of little spiders? Although I had never seen them in their millions, I knew that they must be there because their silk was so plentiful. Neither Father or Mother could enlighten me about the glaggen, so I still don't know. Soon the flowers of the flax dropped off and little round seed boxes like nuts took their place and the flax was ready to harvest. It all had to be hand-pulled but, with very little root, this was not so hard as one might think.

In those days flax went through an awful lot of processing. First it was pulled and bound into sheaves, then it was stooked or built into little round stacks, called martin huts because of their likeness to the houses of some African tribes. A large sheaf of flax was gathered, tied near the top, then opened up umbrella-wise to cover the top of these little stacks. After it had dried a while, the flax was put through a peculiar little threshing mill, which separated the seed-boxes from the stalks, but did not deseed the heads. The heads were taken in bags to a mill in Blairgowrie where they were deseeded, and the stalks were piled into a dam or river to soak for a week or so. After this they were taken out of the dam and spread like a blanket across fields to dry again, before being taken to the mill.

We did not work to any set time, but started and stopped as it suited us best. Nor did we ever have any set times for eating. On very warm days we would stop work during the hottest part of the day. The older men and women would sit talking or have a sleep, and the younger ones would go to the river to bathe and cool off—the women and girls going to a secluded place away from the men and older boys.

Very often the young people would walk as far as five miles to the nearest cinema. They would go in bunches and return all together. Sometimes a young couple would slip away together, or a young boy might want to go to a pub, but the others always had to wait for them so that they all arrived home together. Some parents were very strict, on their daughters especially, and often beat them if they discovered they had been alone with a boy. Money was spent as it was earned, mostly on the children: gold rings and earrings for girls and women, often out of pawnshops. The men dealed about with ponies, carts, and sometimes old cars or lorries. So that although we worked a lot we were none the richer.

Not all travellers were like this, but most were.

34

Came the back end of the year, and the parting of the ways again for us.

Each family would be going to look for somewhere to

erect a winter tent and school their children. This was no easy matter, unless they knew a farmer who needed them. Some travellers went into houses. At that time an old house in a town was not hard to get.

'I am going back to Brechin,' Daddy said one evening as we sat round the fire. He looked towards me as he spoke. 'Well, if you are,' I said, 'then it's cheerio. I will go and bide wi' Bella or one of my aunties. I'm gaen back to nae school.' 'Now look here, lassie, everything is alright. I was doon tae Brechin one of the last days and Mr Anderson, your auld headmaster, wants you to go back to school.' 'Well, he *will* bloody want me!' I almost screamed at Daddy. Tears, rare for me, were stinging my eyes. 'That's the man's thanks for being so good to you,' he said. 'It's nae use, Daddy! I'm no' gaen, I'm no' gaen!' My voice rose louder with every word.

Daddy knew from past experience that I was more stubborn than the mules he had driven during the war, so he heaved one of his deep sighs and turned away, I felt awful for hurting Daddy—that in fact was the reason for the tears—but the thought of going back to school, and facing all those girls, was too much. Much too much. 'Never mind her,' Mother told him. 'What good does education do a body anyway? Ye cannae put wit whaur there's nane, nae matter how much ye educate folk. Too much education is like a big tocher o' money. It can do more harm than good if ye havenae the wit to use it sensibly.'

At this time I was more than perturbed by strange, disturbing sensations which troubled my mind and body. I knew they had something to do with growing up, and sex. But they could not be because I desired sex, I thought—trying to analyse them—because any accidental glimpses of adult male nudity which I had seen had repulsed me. Then what was the meaning of these strange disturbances? Did other girls feel them? I never had the courage to ask. I could not understand them. They completely baffled me and I always got very irritated with things which I could not understand, nor explain. So I was more than hurtful to my poor Mammie and Daddy.

I was really wicked. There is no other word for it. Going

into a mad tantrum, I shouted the cruellest things I could think of. Once I threw a scone which I had been about to eat, hitting Daddy on the face with it. I can still see the look of perplexed astonishment on his dear face. 'I never thought that I would live to see the day,' he said, 'and from you by anybody, Bessie.' I wanted to run to him and plead for his forgiveness, but some little devil's imp held me back. 'I am going to hit her, Maggie, I just couldnae let her off with that.' 'Leave her to me,' Mother told him. Daddy walked away.

I felt tired and shaken after my outburst and filled with hate for myself. I waited for Mother's anger to show, but instead she said 'Here, lassie, fill my pipe for me while I get this rabbit skinned'—handing me her pipe and a git of black bogy-roll tobacco. I took them and began to tease the tobacco with my fingers. I then picked the dottle out of the bottom of the pipe with a hairpin, filled the pipe with the teased tobacco, and put the dottle on the top. This made it easier to light the fresh tobacco.

'Light it for me,' Mother said. 'I mind when I was about your age I nearly killed a cuddy which my father had. I used to go into the town for messages with this wee cuddy, yoked to a wee two-wheeled cart that my father had specially made. We reared this wee cuddy from a foal. My father, seeing how much I liked it, had said to me "Well, tak' it and be good to it." And I was good to it—grooming it, feeding it, speaking to it. I wouldn't have given my wee cuddy for all of the world. But it could be very thrawn and would often sit down on the road and refuse to budge. Now one day when it did this something came over me, and I lifted a larek stick and laid on to it. My father gave me tuppence worth, I can tell you. "You soulless-hearted wee bitch," he said. "walting a poor wee dumb animal that cannae defend itself."

'As I was saying, I was just about your age at the time, and at your age there is a lot going on inside your body which affects your brain as well. This is you changing and leaving childhood behind you. Soon you'll be a young woman. I gret for weeks because I had hurt my wee cuddy, and I ken you will be feeling bad because of what you done to your father.'

'And to you too, Mammie. I'm sorry,' I said, laying my head on her lap and really crying. 'For God's sake, lassie! You're not a wean now. Wheesht!' Mother was stroking my hair as she spoke.

'Stall, hantle binging!' (Stop, there are strange people coming!) 'Halleluja hantle,' Mother continued. She always called the missionaries and other preachers, who often used to come round the camping sites, Halleluja people. I quickly dried my eyes and tried to tidy my hair and pull up my ankle socks. Two women and a man approached rather hesitantly. Although most travellers treated them with respect, there were some who would hurtle abuse at them.

Mother welcomed them, to put them at their ease. 'You have brought a nice day with you,' she sàid. 'Yes, lovely isn't it?' the elder of the two women answered her. 'We have brought some very good news for you too. News of the coming of Jesus Christ. Do you read?' 'No' me,' Mother answered her. 'The lassie here sometimes reads the Bible to me, but I dinnae understand it very weel.' 'Oh, but we will be very happy to explain anything to you that you would like to know.'

'Weel, tell me one thing and tell me no more. That bit about a man named Elijah and one named Elisha. Why, could you tell me, did Elisha curse the wee bairns for calling him old baldie head, and why did God send a wild bear to spall the bairns into pieces?' 'Because these were wicked children, and deserved to be punished.'

'Wicked children?' Mother repeated her words. 'How could an innocent bairn be wicked? And what is wicked about a bairn calling anybody baldie head? Na, na, missus, that's no' my idea of what God is like at a'. Would ye say that that was a God-like thing to do?' 'Oh yes, there are some very wicked children.' The missionary was confident that many children were really very wicked indeed, and that God was justified in having them cruelly killed.

'Weel, tell me this, then. That story about God telling Abraham to tak' his laddie Isaac and burn him to death—what do you think about that?' 'That is easy. God was testing Abraham to find out how much Abraham loved God, and he proved his love for God by showing his willingness to sacrifice his son Isaac.'

I could see that Mother did not think very much of their explanations. 'Do you honestly think that God would need to do the like o' that?' she asked. 'I am only a poor ignorant gan-aboot body, but I would ken the depth of anybody's feelings without testing them like that. Surely God would know better than I would.'

So saying, she dismissed them by telling them that she would have to get on with making the supper. After they had moved on to the next tent Mother said, 'Did ye ever hear the like of that? They ken nae more than I do, and yet they go about preaching to folk. Anybody with any sense at a' would ken that God had nae need to do they things. Whoever wrote these things just put down whatever they thought themselves, I think.'

Just like that Katie came in-about with the two bairns. She had been away for water. Some of the others also came running up to our fireside to avoid having to speak to the Halleluja people. Annie was one of them.

'Where is my Uncle Sandy?' she asked. 'He's awa' for a walk somewhere,' I told her. 'Why are you asking?' 'Weel, my Daddy has gotten three or four dozen tattie sculls to mend, and he wants Uncle Sandy to give him a hand to mend them. That means he will be here for another day or two. I hope he does, because we wouldn't like to be left here ourselves.' 'I hope he does too,' I said. 'He says he is going back to Brechin and I don't want to go back there. Not to the school, anyway.'

'But it has all been cleared up, hasn't it? The lassies were so shocked when one of them was killed by a car that the others owned up to putting the ten-shilling note in your pocket. Imagine folk doing the like of that just because you beat them at lessons. Bad beings, that's what they are. If I were you I would go back and I would show them that I could still beat them a'.' Annie spoke vehemently. 'Not me,' I answered her. 'If anybody covets a thing so much as that, then I want no part of it. Anything coveted so much could bring nothing but bad luck. They can keep their education. I'll survive without it.'

'Oh, Auntie Maggie, the savour of whatever you're cooking is takin' the heart from me. What is it?' Annie turned toward Mother and was peering into the big pan.

Mother had parboiled three tender young rabbits, then jointed them. Now she was frying the joints with onions. She also had a large pot of potatoes ready, mashed and creamed with butter and a little milk. 'Weel, I'm sure there is plenty for us all. Do you see your Uncle Sandy coming yet?' 'Aye, he's down at our tent speaking to my da. I'll run down and tell him that his supper is ready. But mind, I'm coming back for a bit of that rabbit.'

Father looked cheery enough as he came in-about. 'Weel, are all you she-bangs in better moods now?' he asked. Annie answered him, 'And what about he-bangs? Dinnae tell me that they are any better.' She and Daddy joked about for a bit then she asked him 'Are you going to stay with us, Uncle Sandy, to mend the sculls with Daddy?' 'Aye, I have just been telling your father that I will stay on with him. Mebbe Bessie will help us. Will you, Bessie?'

I was so grateful to Daddy for pretending to have forgotten my wild outburst and behaviour, but I only nodded to him. If I'd let my eyes meet his I am sure I would have cried again. 'Now off with you, every one of you,' Mother said, after we had eaten. 'I want a wee minute to myself. Katie, you take Lexy with you, and you take Nancy, Bessie. Bring them back about eight o'clock.'

35

'Come on then, Chookie,' I said. (Chookie was my pet name for little Nancy.) Annie went to get her little brother, for Katie had her own pals that she went with.

Little Nancy was six now and really spoiled: Mother and Father were demented with her. She was forever coming running in-about, screaming that one or other of the other children was hitting her. I'm afraid I was one of the worst for spoiling her. 'Does my wee Chookie want a cuddy-back?' I asked her, looking into her lovely blue eyes which seemed to be studded with little twinkling stars. I knelt down and she jumped on to my back, then I started pretending to gallop and prance, making her scream with laughter.

'I wonder if the hazel nuts are ready now?' I said to Annie, as she approached with her wee brother. He was kicking her shins because she wouldn't give him chewing gum out of her mouth. 'I cannae give you it, Robin, out of my dirty mouth. I'll get you some tomorrow.' He was about the same age as Nancy and his real name was Duncan. 'I just thought you would want to go down by the burn,' Annie said to me. 'You are the awfullest lassie for burns that I ever seen.'

So down to the burnside we went, and the hazel nuts were ready. Does any product of the earth grow more beautifully than hazel nuts, I thought, as I looked at them. Lovely little clusters set into little green florets. We filled our pockets, socks and little Nancy's pinafore with the clusters— to take back to the tents with us.

On our way back we went into Mary's and Johnnie's tent. Mary was feeding her baby, and I marvelled at the difference in her since she had first come amongst us. She and Johnnie had their own way of doing now. That is to say that they had their own fire and that Mary was doing the cooking for herself and Johnnie. Often, indeed more than often, young married couples were still treated as children. They lived with either the boy's or the girl's parents, and they all mucked in together—until the parents were satisfied that they were capable of running their own lives and, above all, looking after the children. This was especially important where a boy had married a scaldie.

'Where are you going tomorrow?' Mary asked. 'We are staying on for a day or two,' Annie told her, 'and so is Bessie's folk.' 'I don't know where to go,' Mary said. 'It is so hard to get a place to settle for the winter.'

'How did you like Aberdeenshire?' I asked her. 'Oh, it was fine. The people are ever so friendly, but I couldn't understand a word they were saying at first. I was going out selling clothes pegs, and every house I went to the women would say Willie Whyte this or Willie Whyte that. I was always telling Johnnie that some fellow named Willie Whyte always seemed to be on the same road and taking the same houses as I was. What a laugh he got at me when he discovered that the folk were saying "Weel-awyte", meaning "Certainly"! I could have sworn they were saying Willie Whyte!'

Annie and I laughed, and stayed to talk a little longer with Mary, and we shared the hazel nuts with her. Wee Nancy was playing outside with Ricky. 'Come on, Chookie!' I called to her. Annie left us and went to her own tent.

When we got to our tent Mother was washing little Lexy's hair. Almost immediately little Nancy started to cry 'I don't want my hair washed!' The little girls hated to have their long hair washed, because Mother always poured a kettle full of cold water over their heads as a last rinse. This was to close the pores, she said, and to keep them from catching the cold. But it is an awful feeling, after having your hair washed in nice warm water, to have cold water poured over your head.

Daddy was sitting splitting cane which Uncle Jimmie had bought in an ironmonger's. The cane was to mend the farmer's potato baskets. I looked at him and caught his eyes and was ever so pleased to see that the pain, caused by my previous bad behaviour, was gone. It had still been there when I left, in spite of Daddy's joking and apparent good humour. Now his eyes were tender and a little sad. 'My bairn is growing up,' he said, and I knew that Mother had been talking to him about me. I crept over and leaned against his knee, 'Daddy...,' I began—but he cut in, saying 'Watch yourself with that cane. It could cut you to the bone. Would you like to roll it up after I have split it?'

I knew that he had cut in to stop me from apologising to him. We understood each other, and were both content.

36

'Here's the farmer coming,' Mother said, hastily endeavouring to tidy up around the fire. The farmer was quite a young man. 'Ah, there you are, Sandy,' he said. 'I see you are getting ready to mend my sculls.' Daddy rose up. He respected his farmer, who was very fair and never came and ordered any of us about.

Travellers, especially the men, hate to be ordered about. In fact they just will not take it. They would just up and away. I think this is one of the reasons why they would never take on work other than piece-work. Another reason is that they hate to be tied down in any way. Any farmer familiar with travellers, especially a fruit farmer, will tell you that twenty travellers could do the work of a hundred country hantle—if they are just left to get on with it. This is not boasting. It is true. I know travellers who can each pick over three hundredweights of raspberries in a day, or five tons of potatoes. Of course this is not true of all work, but they can more than hold their own in most jobs.

'Yes, Mr Mathers, I am just getting the cane ready,' Father told the farmer.

'A lot of you are gan awa' the morn, I hear,' the farmer said. 'Aye, there's just my brother Jimmie and me staying. Was there anything that you needed done like?' Father asked him.

'Well, I have the threshing mill coming tomorrow and I could have done wi' a few of you. I'll need twa men onyway. One for the leading. Can you or your brother bigg a cart or a stack?' Father smiled, saying 'I think so.' 'Ah, weel, that's fine.' The farmer continued 'I'll also need twa women for the lousin', and somebody for the chaff. In fact, I could have done wi' somebody tae piet as weel but you have nae young lads, Sandy.'

'No, mair the pity,' Father answered him, 'but maybe Bessie here could piet. My wife and Katie can do the lousin' and Jimmie's lassie Annie will dae the chaff.' The farmer looked at me, asking 'Do you think you would manage, lass?' 'I'll try my best,' I answered.

So next day there I was standing on a ladder halfway up a stack, and with a pitchfork doing what was called pieting. The man who had brought the cart, laden with sheaves from the harvest field, forked them up to me. I had to catch them off his pitchfork with my pitchfork then fork them up to the man who was building the stack.

(I must point out here that my work had nothing to do with the threshing, lest you older farm workers will think that I am blethering. No, they were rather belatedly threshing some stacks from the previous year's harvest away over at the other side of the stackyard.)

However, I was allowed to join the threshers in partaking of the lovely food which the farmer's wife, with the help of her maid and a cottar woman, had prepared for the workers. This was a customary and, I think, traditional thing. Always when the threshing mill came to a farm the workers were all given a good meal. Bottles of beer were also supplied for the men, women too, if they desired it. Although pieting was hard work I was happier than I would have been on the threshing mill. It was too noisy.

Aunt Edna had been looking after Lexy and Nancy for us, and she also had a nice cup of tea ready for us all when we got home. I went to bed early that night and, as I stretched myself out on my bed of straw, I realised how tired I was. Pleasantly tired, almost ecstatically tired—if you can imagine anyone being ecstatically tired—but I have no other word for the way I felt. So I was soon asleep.

The next morning was spent bidding farewell to our friends and relations. As usual this was a very emotional time. I felt it most after they were away, when I looked at the marks where their tents had been.

I spent the rest of that day helping to mend the farmer's sculls, and walked with Annie in the evening. As we approached the tents on the way home, Annie sniffed and said 'Your mother is surely baking bannocks. I'm coming along to get one.' The bannocks were set upright on an iron grid a good bit back from the fire, which was made entirely of broom wood. Broom was the only wood that would not 'taste' the bannocks with its smoke.

Katie was away to Blair Atholl, with Uncle Willie and his family. She had pleaded to be allowed to go, as she would miss the girls so much. Travellers mostly follow their hearts. They think it is very stupid for people who love each other to be apart—for any reason. Katie would have been lonely and miserable when the girls left, but we knew that she would not stay long away. Her devotion for her parents and indeed for all of us was too strong.

As Annie and I climbed over the dyke to where the tents were, we disturbed a lizard which had been lying on top of the dyke. It hastened away leaving its tail wriggling about on the grass at the foot of the dyke. 'You silly wee thing, I would not hurt you,' I said. 'Oh, shaness! The tail is alive!' Annie shouted. 'Look! Look at it moving by itself! What did you pull off its tail for anyway?' 'I never pulled its tail off. It just came off itself. Mebbe it's not a tail, mebbe it's one just newly born and its legs will grow later like a puddock does.' Annie asked Uncle Jimmie when we reached their tent and he laughed at our excitement, and told us that lizards throw off their tails to distract people and animals who might hurt them.

Although we children worked a lot with our parents, there was no compulsion. We did it voluntarily. We could stop and go and play any time that we wanted to.

On a warm day Annie and I always stopped and went to the river or to a burn, where we would find a secluded spot, strip, and wash ourselves and our hair. We liked to sit in the middle of the shallow rapids on a stone. We would often sit there for hours on end. Sometimes we took the washing with us and it would be dry by the time we came out of the water. Sometimes we took the bairns with us and bathed them in the burn—but we liked better to be by ourselves so that we could relax, and be free to enjoy ourselves.

Mother had once told us that the water of the River Isla contained some special quality which could make even the plainest girl beautiful, unless she had really some truly bad features like an enormous nose or such, which water couldn't wash away. 'If you tell us that we will go and put a tent up on the banks of the Isla and lie in the water all day,' we girls had told her. 'I'm not joking,' she said, 'this is supposed to be true.' Anyway we never got a chance to challenge her word, never being long enough beside the Isla.

Sometimes Annie and I would take the ponies to the river for a drink, sitting on their backs, but we were never allowed to ride them on the roads unless someone had them by the head. Father liked to keep young fiery animals which were inclined to be highly strung and might bolt without a strong hand. He just could not be happy with a horse which was too quiet and stolid. So he was not over-keen on us riding them.

We finished mending the potato baskets in four days. It was still September and Mother asked Father to take her up the country, before going back to Brechin. 'I was intending to tak' you anyway,' Father answered. 'I know you are ettling to go to Blair Atholl to see how Hendry is now.'

Hendry had left us some three weeks earlier, still looking a bit peekish. 'I'll never be able to repay you, Uncle and Aunt,' he had said, crying and kissing them, 'I would have died but for you. I'll never forget what you have done, never.' 'You can start repaying us now,' Mother had told him, 'by looking after yourself and never letting yourself get into such a state again.' 'I will start, Aunt Maggie, I will—I promise you.'

Uncle Jimmie and family decided to come with us, and I was so pleased to have the company of Annie.

37

So we took the road the next morning, Annie and I walking behind the yokes. We stopped at the common in Coupar Angus to let Mother and Edna go to the shops.

'Bessie, go and see if you can get some boiling water. I am dying for a mouthful of tea.' 'Well, you had better watch the weans,' I answered Daddy, 'and Annie can come with me.' The bairns were playing on the swings. 'Here! take these coppers with you,' Daddy said. 'You can offer to pay them for the boiling water,' and he handed me three pennies. So Annie and I set off to get the tea made, not taking the tea can but another big milk can. I passed the big houses and chose a row of little single-ends, knowing that the occupants would be more tolerant. The very first door I knocked at was opened by a young girl of perhaps nineteen.

She was heavy with child, but there was little but skin on the rest of her body.

'I am sorry,' she said, 'my fire is out.' 'I am the one who is sorry,' I said. 'I would never have troubled you if I'd known you were not well.' 'Oh, it's not that,' she said. 'I am pleased that you came to my door, but I just have no way of boiling water for you.' She was obviously embarrassed yet somehow reluctant to let us leave.

Then I caught her eyes and seldom have I seen such a deep expression of despair and hurt, mingled with fear.

'If you have gas I will give you money to put in the meter,' I told her. 'We always give people a penny for the gas if they boil water for us,' I lied. 'Can we come in?' I was determined to try and help this girl so, without waiting for her reply, I walked past her into the room. She came in behind Annie, who by her whispered reprovals in cant was making it obvious to me that she thought I was being rather bold. 'Where is your meter?' I asked the girl. 'Under the sink,' she replied. There was a gas ring on top of the fireplace so I filled her kettle, lit the gas after putting a penny in the meter, and put the kettle on.

I quickly scanned the room. There was nothing in it belonging to a man. 'You are far from your native home,' I said to the girl, who had sat down looking very tired and weary. 'Yes, I come from Newcastle, but I have been up here for four years.' 'You are not married,' I boldly told her. She blushed and shook her head.

'Do you get any money to keep you?' I asked her. 'I've worked since I came out of school, and never missed a day. Yet they won't give me one penny off my stamps.' 'But why?' I asked. 'Surely you're entitled to the dole?' She went to a drawer, took out a letter from the Labour Exchange, and handed it to me. It stated that she was not entitled to benefit because she was unavailable for work.

'Have you tried the parish?' I asked her. 'Yes, but they told me to see the baby's father or to go home to my people. My mother's dead, and she never was married. I had some money saved, but I've been three months off work.'

'Have you no friends to help you?' Annie asked. 'What about the boy's parents?' 'Oh no, I just couldn't.' The girl was beyond tears, like someone already dead, with only the body alive.

'We'll have to go before this tea gets cold,' I told her 'but we will come back again.' 'When?' she asked, with eyes that implored us. 'Just shortly after we have our tea.'

As Annie and I walked back to the common she said 'Poor lassie, but mebbe she is a shan dilly.' 'Away!' I answered her. 'If she was a shan dilly she would not need to be hungry or want other things.'

Mother and Edna had returned from the shops, and they were all waiting on us coming with the tea. 'What kept you two?' Uncle Jimmie asked. 'Oh, you can depend that it was Bessie,' Father told him. 'That lassie cannae see a midge passing but she has to examine it.'

'Daddy dear,' I said, 'if you had seen what we have seen you wouldn't be able to take any tea.' 'What did you see?' he asked. Annie was anxious to tell them, so I let her go ahead.

'Oh, Uncle Sandy, a poor young lassie and she is not the thickness of a thread, and her belly is to her mouth.' They laughed. 'If she is not the thickness of a thread, how can her belly be to her mouth?' Uncle Jimmie asked her. 'Ach, ye ken what I mean,' she said. 'She is not married, and there is not as much as a crumb of bread nor anything that she would get tuppence for in the house.'

Mother and Edna were a bit away from where we were sitting. They were feeding the children. The children always got first, then the men, then the women and girls. Edna called us over. 'I thought youse were dying for a mouthful of tea,' she shouted. 'It doesn't look like it!'

As we sat down beside them, Father said to the two women 'They two lassies are going on about something. Will you go and see after you get your tea?' Annie and I then told Mother and Edna. We were all sitting in a circle now, the ponies relieved of the weight of the carts but, still harnessed, were munching the grass. They would be given a drink before we moved on.

After the two women had smoked, they said 'You two lassies tidy up the place and wash the dishes, and tell us where this lassie bides that you were talking about.' We directed them to the door, and went to do as we were bid.

There was a water tap at the entrance to the green. Soon we had the place looking as if we had never been there, while the children rolled about on the grass and the men talked. Then we sat down beside our fathers.

Suddenly I saw Father's face changing colours—first deathly white and then fiery red. I turned around to see the cause and saw a policeman coming striding across the common towards us. 'That's the whore's son that put the boot to Hendry,' Uncle Jimmie said. 'Aye, that's him with the bullock eyes and the blabber mouth.' The policeman approached us almost shouting 'It's about bloody high time that you lads were out of here! What the hell are you doing sitting there all day? You should be all made gang and work like other folk. There is ower mony of your kind gan aboot. Come on, get yoked up and get to hell out of here.'

Father and Uncle Jimmie looked so composed, but I could tell by the tremor of Father's hands that he was having difficulty restraining himself. He was afraid to speak as if by the very act of speaking he might be spurred to fly at the policeman.

So he stuck out his tongue and put his finger to it and then to his backside, cocking his leg as he did so. Uncle Jimmie couldn't suppress his laughter and Annie and I ran round the other side of the carts giggling uncontrollably. Jimmie spoke in cant, telling Father not to do anything that he could get jailed for.

The policeman was boiling mad. 'Less of your bloody cheek, shut up that gibberish, and get going, you dirty orra-looking buggers.' Father repeated his action with his finger, whereat the policeman made as if to jump on him, saying 'You're coming with me to jail!'

Father jumped up and spoke for the first time. 'If you just wait for about five minutes I will be ready to go to jail,' he said. 'I am just going to do something worth going to jail for. I am going to put you on your back for at least six months, if not into your coffin. Then I'll gladly go to the gallows. It's no' a poor, sick, paralytic drunk laddie that you are up against now, you dirty bull-bitch's son. You are a big clever chap, eh? A disgrace to the King's uniform! That's what you are. Too many of our kind is there? Well it's a bloody good job there is not many of your kind. Come on then! I thought you were going to take me to the jail. I'm ready for you. Come! I cannae wait to get into jail!'

The policeman's bullock eyes were nearly out of his head and his blubber lip was trembling with the power of rage—but he turned on his heel and left, shouting 'I'll be back, and then you will see what you will get for insulting the law!' He looked back now and then lest Father would jump on him from behind.

'Go and see what's keeping your mothers,' Uncle Jimmie said to Annie and me. 'I'll bet he is away to phone the tobies in Blair or Perth even. We will all be quadded. If they women would only come we could be away before they come.' Uncle Jimmie was a bit scared.

'If you wait I'm going to run like a rabbit,' Father said. 'No, I'm staying where I am. Anyway the polis in Blair have cars and so do the Perth ones. If we run they will soon find us. He can do nothing to us. Our word is as good as his, and this is common ground. What harm are we doing sitting, taking a drop tea? This common ground belongs to everybody.'

When Annie and I got to the girl's house there was no-one there.

'Where do you think they have gone?' I asked. 'God knows,' Annie replied. 'We had better just go back and wait for them.'

The police from Blairgowrie arrived, accompanied by the village one, before our mothers did—and as God would have it one of them was a sergeant who had known Daddy for years, and Jimmie also.

'Oh, it's you, is it, Sandy? What's this you have been doing to Constable Wallace?'

'Me?' said Father. 'Ye ken fine, sergeant, that I never gave a wrong word to a policeman in my life. When he asked us to move on, I only told him that we would have to wait for the women coming. Whar would I say anything to the law?'

He looked Blubber Lips square in the eye as he said this last sentence. The blubber lips started spilling a storm of abuse and spittle, and the bullock eyes again threatened to jump out of his head. 'Sergeant, between you and me I think that Constable Wallace is an unwell man. Poor soul, he doesn't look well to me,' Father continued.

'Arrest them, take the whole bloody lot of them! Where the hell are your bloody women? Away begging and pestering the folk of the village, I'll bet.' Constable Wallace was almost foaming at the mouth.

The sergeant said 'I cannot arrest folk for sitting drinking tea.'

'So you are taking the word of them damned tinks before mine,' Wallace went on. 'You are just as bloody bad as what they are. I'll get some of the buggers anyway! I'll go and find the women and charge them for begging.' So saying he hurried away across the common.

'Now then, Sandy, what is all this about? I wasn't born today or yesterday and I know that you must have been saying something to Constable Wallace,' the sergeant asked. 'I cannot take you in because he was alone, but I will give you the benefit of the doubt, as you are—as you say—not one for breaking the law much.'

'Well, sergeant, I have no proof either, but I am not joking when I tell you that that man should go for treatment to some lunatic asylum. I am no' very wise mysel', but I wouldn't have that man's conscience for a thousand pounds.' Father didn't want to be too hard on Constable Wallace. It just wasn't in his nature. So he refrained from telling them about Hendry. 'I just hope he doesn't get too cheeky with my wife or I'll be sorry for him,' Father continued.

The two policemen laughed. 'Is she a tartar, Sandy?' 'She is much more than that,' he answered, without joining in their laughter. 'We will go and see if we can find him and tell him to leave the women alone. Where are you making for tonight?' 'It will have to be Meikleour or maybe Spittalfield. I ken farmers there that will let us stay the night. I am going up to Blair Atholl.' 'Well, we will hang about till we see the women back, but if Wallace has arrested them for begging there is nothing we can do about it.' 'My wife never begged in her life,' Father told him. 'If she gets anything from anybody she usually gives them good value for it. A basket, clothes pegs, or some sma' thing like thread or needles. So I have no fear o' that.'

After the police left Jimmie asked, 'What in the name of God is keeping they women anyway? Go back, youse lassies, and look for them again. It will be night before we get moving.'

There was still no-one in the young girl's house, and Annie and I were beginning to think that perhaps Wallace *had* arrested our mothers. Then we spotted them and the girl coming out of the local parish office. The girl's face was alive again. She ran to meet us saying 'Look! I've got twelve and sixpence plus a seven-and-six line for messages! And, more than that, your mothers have arranged for me to be taken into the Salvation Army home to have my baby. Even more than that they bought me loads of food. I am packed to the gullet!'

'Aye, and even more than that, they have had you into the pub,' I told her. She nodded, saying 'Yes, they gave me two milk stouts.'

'And had a couple of nips apiece themselves, by the look of them,' Annie joined in, laughing. 'We must hurry Ma,' I said. 'Daddy is not in a very good humour.' The girl thanked them and us, and we left her at her door.

'Ma, you had better put a couple of they cloves in your mouth, and give Edna some too.' Mother always carried cloves in her pocket. Some days she would weary for a pint of stout or something, and the cloves put the smell of drink away. She had worked very hard all her life and she deserved this little extra sustenance, but today it might just be enough to set up a battle royal between her and Father. 'What's ado with him then?' Mother asked us. 'Because we have taken so lang?' 'Oh, it's more than that, but he'll tell you about it himself.'

38

Travellers often helped people who were really down as that young girl had been.

If no money was coming into a house the scaldies suffered much more than we did, as few of them could turn their hand to anything that would bring in a few coppers. In particular young girls with infants, whose husbands had walked out, or who had never been married. Motherhood without marriage was considered a great disgrace, and mothers would often try to hide the fact that their daughters were with child. Sometimes tinkers would acquire children born out of wedlock. Mothers desperate to conceal that their daughter had a child would give the infant to some tinker. Those bairns were reared as their own—but told at a very early age, so that they would not be hurt by someone telling them when they grew up.

Traveller women, too, supplied a great number of poor cottars, and also townswomen, with clothes. Travelling from door to door the traveller women would often receive lots of quite good clothing and anything that was no use to themselves, or their own family, they would sell for a few pence or exchange for food. Often, as a child, I had seen lots of children wearing clothes which their mothers had gotten from my mother. It used to irk me when they started shouting 'Tinkie, tinkie, torn rags!' at me, and them wearing clothes they had got from a 'tinkie'. However, we traveller children kept quiet—as this was always a source of income.

Mother and Edna were in high spirits as we approached the common, laughing and joking as they walked. I noticed the police car passing us slowly then, with gathering speed, turning into the Blairgowrie road. I knew that Father would still be in rather a gurly mood so I tried to prepare Mother, as nothing seemed to get her back up so quickly as someone throwing a damper on her when she was in cheerful mood.

'Daddy's no' very happy with himsel',' I told her. 'What's wrang wi' him?' she asked. 'I suppose he's fed up waiting for you,' I told her. 'It's two o'clock in the day, Ma.

You have been away for hours.' 'I *am* bad about him,' she answered. 'His brother will likely be cooking his horns too,' Edna put in.

'In the name of God, women, what kept you so long?' were Daddy's first words. 'If some dirty wee tail cannae keep her legs together she deserves a' that's coming to her.' 'Were you no' the one that told me to go?' Mother retorted. I left them, and Uncle Jimmie and Edna, all bickering together and went to fetch the bairns who were romping about with Ricky some distance away.

Soon we were ready for the road again. We had decided to go no further than Meikleour that day. A number of other travelling families were staying on the camping ground waiting for the potato harvest to begin: McDonalds, Reids and McLarens. They were strangers to me, but known to Mother and Father. The women made tea for us all and shared their food with our children. The men helped Father and Uncle Jimmie to erect the tents, talking and questioning each other about their forbears and acquaintances. There were hordes of children of all ages. After all our bellies had been filled with the evening meal, we all started getting really acquainted.

All the ponies were inspected by the men and exchanges made. Daddy exchanged our rather fiery young horse for one less spirited and more docile, warning the new owner about the things that it shied at. Mother was not very happy about the few shillings Father had accepted in the bargain. 'That animal you got is ewe-necked,' she told Father. 'Ewe-necked or not,' Father answered her, 'I will not have to walk, or jump off the cart to grip it by the head every minute of the day. This one is much safer for the bairns.'

The women soon all got together, newsing and cracking, while the children played. Annie and I went walking to where we were told the well was, taking the horses' pails with us as well as our own clean pails.

As we walked along Annie gave a startled cry. Feathers and pieces of a bird had dropped down on top of her. 'A hawk, surely,' I said, as we both looked up. 'That's the queerest thing that I have ever seen,' Annie continued. 'There's not a sign of a hawk or any other bird of prey.' We were still both looking up when suddenly we saw a gull disintegrate in mid-air, and more feathers came floating down. 'God bless me, that is queer,' I said, inspecting the feathers.

Then we heard someone giggling in some bushes. We ran towards the bushes and came upon two young boys of about fifteen years of age. They had a carbide cycle lamp and some bread, and were busy rolling the bread into balls after putting a piece of carbide in the centre. They then threw the balls of bread for the birds to pick up.

My temper arose instantly and I flew at one of the boys, grabbing him firmly by the hair with my two hands and hurtling words of abuse at him. To give him his due, he tried frantically to loosen my fingers before hitting me, provoked by the pain of his head. He was a big strong boy and I was literally swinging from his hair. His first punch sent me reeling into the bushes, but he came with me, my hands still gripping his hair. His punch had landed at the root of my ear and I was stunned a bit. Luckily he hadn't fallen on top of me as we had gone down sideways. Soon, however, he got the better of me and sat with his knees on top of my shoulders—holding me down.

He was about to give me another punch when Annie rushed in and put one of the galvanised buckets over his head. The other boy was enjoying the whole thing and going into fits of laughter. Annie was trying to keep the boy's head in the bucket and, in his efforts to get at her, his knee-holds on me slackened and I wriggled free, jumping to my feet. The boy, too, was soon on his feet having thrown Annie and the bucket aside. 'I'll rip you with a kick,' he told me, 'if you come near me again.' He was holding his head. I looked at his tackety boots, but so intense was my fury that I was just about to charge him again when we heard a voice shouting.

The other boy looked around, then took to his heels towards the encampment. The voice belonged to one of three young men who had come out of the wood. 'My God Almighty, Robbie, that's no' you fighting with a lassie?' 'Eh, ye dirty cowardly pup that you are, wait till I tell your father about ye.' Another of the young men was speaking.

They had been away hunting with their dogs and were carrying hares and rabbits.

'That's no' a lassie,' the boy shouted. 'That's some kind of she-devil! She is the one that has been doing all the fighting. My brains are bouncing with her swinging on my hair.' 'God bless me, min, you should be ashamed of yourself, hitting a wee bit lassie.' The young men were really giving him gyp. 'Come on, lassies, and we will help you get your water and carry it hame for you,' one of them said.

I had calmed down a bit now, and had found my voice again. 'Dinnae bother telling his father,' I said. 'He is speaking the truth. I wouldn't leave him alone. I was angry at him for killing the birds.' I washed my face and tried to tidy my hair at the stream down from where the well was. I noticed at the same time the admiring looks which Annie, who looked more than her thirteen years, was getting from the young men.

The sound of bagpipes wafted across the moor as we made our way home. 'Aye, aye, nae wonder you took so long with the water,' Uncle Jimmie greeted us when we reached the tents, smiling as he spoke. Annie and I both behaved a little unusually, because of our carry-on with the young boy—both of us blushing and unable to answer Uncle Jimmie with our usual cheeky answer to his joke.

An unsmiling Edna rushed at Annie and grabbed her by the hair. 'What have you been up to?' she shouted at her. 'You dirty wee midden!' At this point my mother came out of her tent. Uncle Jimmie slapped Edna's face and released Annie's hair from her hand. 'You don't see Maggie doing that to her lassie,' he said to Edna. 'No, but maybe she should,' Edna retorted. 'Her lassies keep a funny carry-on, tigging and toying wi' laddies.'

Mother turned on her angrily. 'Aye, mebbe,' she said, 'but it's no' the rattling cart that coups first. I'll bet you were as quiet as a wee pussy cat when you were a lassie!' Edna paled, having no desire to cross swords with Mother. She ran into her tent.

Mother scanned Annie and me from tip to toe. 'What were the two of you doing anyway?' she asked. I knew that

Mother was expert at detecting lies so I just told her the truth. 'Lassie, lassie,' she said to me, 'you will have to try and conquer that temper of yours. That laddie could have killed you and you would have had nobody but yourself to blame.'

Uncle Jimmie was still hovering around. He dreaded a fight between the two women. Mother sensed this and decided to try and make it up with Edna without losing face. 'Bairns would be the death of you,' she said to Uncle Jimmie, loud enough for Edna to hear.

'Are you there, Edna?' she called. 'The carry-on wi' they two lassies made me forget what I came out to ask you.' Edna came out of the tent saying 'I was just happing the wean.' 'Would you show me again what way you make that wee scallops round the edges of this?' Mother asked her. Edna crocheted the most beautiful lace doilies and she had been teaching Mother how to make them. Soon the two women were close friends again.

'I'm gan awa' tae hae a crack with some of the men,' Uncle Jimmie told us. 'Bessie, your father wants you to play a wee tune to them. Do you and Annie want to come down with me? Your father is down there now.' 'Oh, Uncle Jimmie, not tonight,' I answered him. I was tired and still drumly after my outburst of temper. I knew that I couldn't concentrate on playing. It always did, and still does, take me a day or two to recover after a fit of temper. Luckily my temper fits have been very rare indeed for many years now.

'Come on,' he said, 'we will hae a hooch and a dance and you will feel better after it. The men are just dying to hear you.' 'No, I just cannae the night, Uncle, and dinnae mention about me fighting wi' that laddie.'

Annie was sitting very quiet and staring vacantly at the fire. We could see that her mother's distrust had hurt her deeply. Edna had never acquired the travelling people's knack of making their children feel happy again after an outburst. Nor did she have the sensitivity to understand completely Annie's feelings.

Uncle Jimmie, however, was different. Going over to Edna he rumpled her hair and kissed her jaw where he had slapped her. Then, taking his pipe from his pocket, he gave it to her, saying 'Here, you can keep it till I come back.' (They always used one pipe between them.) He then looked down at Annie and sighed deeply. 'Do you want to come with me, Blackie?' he asked her. Annie just shook her head without looking up. He then found my eyes and looked at Annie again, then back to me. I nodded slightly, understanding that he wanted me to try and comfort her.

I went and piled a heap of sticks on to the fire, saying 'It's getting chilly.' I knew that the intense heat would force Annie to move and that her irritation at me would shift other things out of her head for the moment anyway. 'Are you trying to roast me?' she said, rising up angrily. 'No, I am not trying to roast you,' I replied. 'I need you too much. I just must go some place and I am feared to go alone.' It was beginning to get dark by now.

'Please, Annie, hurry! I cannae wait much longer.' 'God pity you,' she retorted. 'What would you do if I wasn't here?' 'I'd have to get a cork,' I said, and she laughed in spite of herself.

We walked away towards the wood and Annie spoke about her mother. 'Why does she think so badly of me?' she asked. 'I think she hates me.' 'No, no, Annie, she loves you so much that she is afraid of anything happening to you.' I knew immediately that I had said the wrong thing.

'Then why is your mother not like that with you?' she asked. 'Well now, that's easy. You are so nice-looking, Annie, and so nice-built, and you look all of sixteen. Your mother knows how difficult it is going to be for you.' 'Why? Why? Even if what you say is true?' 'Well, you will have hundreds more temptations than a plain girl. If I looked like you my mother would be as bad as yours is.' I was lying now. My mother would know, I was sure of that, but she would understand and be gentle.

However, Annie was accepting this and I kept talking about things that she would have to listen to and answer, so that her mind did not get a chance to wander. Then I gradually swung the conversation round to other things so that she had almost rid her mind of it all before we returned to the fire.

A number of other women were sitting around the fire

talking to Mother and Edna. Little Lexy had fallen asleep on Mother's knee and Nancy was sitting leaning on Mother, her eyes going together with sleep. 'Put this wean into her bed, Bessie, then put on the kettle for a cup of tea.' I gently lifted the child and undressed and bedded her without wakening her. She just grunted a wee bit in protest at being disturbed. Nancy was sleeping on Mother's knee now, and three of the other women had sleeping weans on their knees too. The women were all talking, each one eager to get her word in.

Annie had put on the kettle and we listened to the women. Their talk was all about people and the things that they had done; people whom they had not seen for a long time and people who were long dead. Then they started to talk about their husbands. One could learn more about a man by listening to his wife talk of him, than one could from knowing him a lifetime. They sat there smoking, drinking tea, and newsing until the small hours of the morning, while children listened—and eventually fell asleep.

Sleep did not come easily to me that night. My brain was still drumly, but very much awake. All sorts of thoughts flashed through my head. So I did as Father had told me. I repeated the Lord's Prayer slowly and concentrated on it. Soon my body relaxed and my brain followed suit and I slept till ten o'clock the next day.

Mother had let me sleep. She had been long up and had a line of washing done. 'Are we staying here another night?' I asked her. 'Aye, but we will have to push on tomorrow,' she answered.

That evening we all had a really good ceilidh. There was a lot of drink going and everybody enjoyed themselves.

39

The next night we stayed at Pitlochry, in a quarry near the town. We spent three nights there, just enjoying ourselves and meeting lots of Mother's relatives.

Little Lexy had the wind taken out of her sails there.

She was forever running to Daddy, Mother or me, crying and saying that this or that child was hitting her. Daddy was a bit fed up with it. So that evening he said to Mother 'Maggie, you are just cutting a stick to break your own back with. Petting the bairn like that and taking her part. Come on out with Daddy, wean, and show me the big girl who was hitting you.'

Lexy went out eagerly with Daddy, thinking that he was going to check the other girl. 'There she is, Daddy! Her there, look!' she said, pointing to a little girl no bigger than herself. The little girl was ready to take flight but Daddy held out a threepenny bit towards her. 'Here take it,' he said, 'that is for hitting Lexy. Give her the same dose every time you see her.'

This infuriated Lexy and she flew at the other little girl. Daddy pulled them apart, asking Lexy if there were any other little girls who hit her. 'No!' she shouted. 'I can fight any of them!' And from that day she did, too: never coming crying to us.

We carried on to Blair. Atholl and stayed there for a week. When we landed there, I asked where Hendry lived and Annie and I ran to his tent to see him.

He did not hear our approach nor did he see us for a few minutes. He was sitting just inside his tent with a child on each knee and one standing between his legs. His head was thrown back, and he was laughing loudly with his eyes closed. The weans were pulling his ears, eyelashes and nose, and he looked well and happy.

Annie and I joined in the nose and ear pulling. Of course he immediately knew and opened his eyes. 'Oh, Cousin Annie, Cousin Bessie, is your folk here too?' He was so pleased to see us again and we were more than pleased to see him so well. Katie was pleased to see us too.

Uncle Andy was there, and first thing he warned us was to keep the bairns away from an enclosure at the back of his tent. He had a young wild cat, and it was really wild. Father admonished him for keeping it. 'It was just a tiny wee starving creature when I got it,' Uncle Andy said. 'The keeper shot its parents and he didn't know that they had young away in at the root of a tree. The others were dead when I found them. I've nursed it like a bairn, but I will soon have to let it go.' It did not look wild but no-one other than Uncle Andy could handle it.

Mother said that he had a way with animals. The wildest dog or horse was easily subdued by him. When Uncle Andy saw Daddy's new pony, he laughed and laughed. 'My God, min, I wouldn't take five pounds a day and be seen on the road with that animal. What did you do with the garron that I sold you?' 'I could do nothing with it,' Father answered him. 'It was wild like yourself.' 'Oh-ho! You *are* a clever horseman!' Uncle Andy was having his kill laughing at Father.

'We can't all be demon horsemen,' Daddy told him. 'They say that you have the Horseman's Word, and they say that it is a gift from the Devil,' Daddy went on. 'If you heed a' you hear, you can eat a' that you see.' Uncle Andy did not like to be told that he was having anything to do with the Devil. His red moustache bristled and he went on 'It must have been some fool like you that said that. Some half-man that couldn't handle a good horse.'

To hear them one would never guess how close those two brothers were, for they would have died for each other. Yet this is how they went on at each other every time they met.

40

The week passed all too quickly and Annie and I, knowing that we would soon be parted, spent all the time possible together.

The partings came again and the exchange of gifts; tears even, and so much hugging and kissing. I had acquired a little treasure of presents.

Travellers at that time would never leave a loved one with an angry countenance. Anything could happen in seconds, and how would a person feel if something happened to a dear one, and you had last spoken to him or her in anger?

And we just lived one day at a time. If we ever had to mention the next day, or what we might be doing the next day—or next year—we always said 'If God spares us.' Never putting anything in front of us, nor making any plans for the future. Even an expectant mother would never gather a lot of clothes for the coming baby. Other women would keep things for her without telling her. Travellers thought it a great sin to hoard up things or money for an event or thing or person, and believed that the very planning or hoarding would bring death or disaster to the person or project. They were afraid, too, to be selfish—believing that anything that they were selfish with would bring bad luck.

Neither would they want anything which was much coveted. I have heard a man say, after his pony broke a leg in a rabbit hole, 'I might have known that I would have no luck with that pony. I should have given it to John when he wanted it.' This is rather a difficult way of thinking to explain.

Some traveller men even felt this way about their wives, forbidding them to make the most of their prettiness lest another man should be envious. So one had to be very careful not to admire anything too much. This was greatly feared, especially when a barren women coveted a child.

I remember one time when I was out 'taking the doors' with my sister Bella. It was a lovely day and we had Bella's children with us. We were in high spirits, singing and laughing as we went.

Bella went to a big house and the woman, about forty-ish, was very nice and greatly admired the children. Then she said 'Are all five of them yours? You look so young.' 'Yes, they are all mine,' Bella answered. 'I am one of those unfortunate women who can't have a child,' the woman continued. 'I have all of this estate and no child of my own to give it to. If you would give me that little boy, he would own all this one day. I am sure you would not miss one of them.'

I saw Bella's face pale, and fear come into her eyes. She grabbed the little boy from the woman's arms and said, 'Come, hurry avree!' to me. The woman was saying 'Don't go! I will give you a lot of money for him.'

We hurried as fast as we could with the children until we reached the encampment, where Bella collapsed sobbing on Mother's shoulder. Bella was a child again. 'Oh, Mammie, Mammie, a woman put her eye on my wean.' Mother tried to comfort her, but I noticed that she too paled at Bella's words. 'The dirty stupit barren mare. Are you sure she put her eye on him?' 'Oh, Mammie, I am sure. Oh Mammie, Mammie, what am I going to do?'

In spite of constant attention and every care, little Donald died that winter. Bella was very composed and quiet. She had already shed all the tears possible and suffered the deepest grief. Always I will remember the look in that woman's eyes. Not just a natural envy or desire, or longing, but some deeper devil-sent emotion.

So you will understand why a traveller wants nothing that is greatly coveted, and why they are much afraid of envy.

Neither do they want anything belonging to the dead. Everything of theirs is burnt. Not money of course: it is given to those who have most need of it. Sometimes a ring or earrings is kept, but only by those who loved the deceased and whom the deceased loved. If a daughter-in-law did not get on very well with her mother-in-law she would not accept anything belonging to her when she died, having a strange belief that the spirit of the dead woman would be angry and seek revenge.

Travellers are absolutely horrified to see the way that scaldies will squabble about things belonging, perhaps, to a dead parent or to some other dear one. Few travellers put much value on any material thing. They like to have them as well as anyone else, but don't worry one bit if they are taken from them or if they lose them. I have never heard of any traveller committing suicide because of material things.

41

But to get back to my story.

We left Blair Atholl and travelled leisurely down country again, reluctant to leave behind all our kindred. All the way I seldom talked and just did as I was asked so obediently and quietly that Father and Mother were demented with me. I just did not want to return to Brechin. And they missed their boisterous, lively, high-spirited daughter.

'Bessie,' Daddy said one day, 'don't think that I am going down to Brechin without a reason. 'Look,' he said, taking a key from his pocket, 'when I was down at Brechin, seeing what they were going to do about the ten shillings you were supposed to steal, they gave me this key. They have given us a beautiful new council house. The workmen were still in it when I was down. It is really nice with a bathroom and garden.' 'Daddy, if they give us Blair Castle I would still not go back to school.' 'You are thrawn,' he said.

'There is something else, Bessie, your mother is expecting a wean.' This stunned me. Old people did not have babies and Mother, at forty-two, was ancient to me. 'Now will you behave yourself and stop thrawing with us?'

'Could I not go and stay with Aunt Liza or Bet?' I asked him. 'I will need you, Bessie, to help me. I am not going to let your mother do anything at all.' 'Daddy, listen. If anyone comes asking for me, about schooling I mean, tell them that I am away living with relations somewhere. I will hide from them all winter. I can easy do it. The days are short.' Daddy shook his head and laughed. 'You are determined not to go back to school. We will see how we get on,' he said.

So we came into Brechin at night early that October and stayed the first night in the old house. The new house was indeed lovely and Daddy soon furnished it, buying things very cheaply at roups and other sales. So that winter I spent a lot of time dodging school.

Mother lost the child she was carrying, and nearly lost her life with it. Daddy couldn't concentrate on doing anything. He just sat by Mother until she got better.

Katie and I endeavoured to keep the house by doing odd jobs for farmers around the town. Sometimes I would wade the river to get to those farms, and cross fields and ditches, lest anyone would see me. Katie was not such a tomboy as me, and didn't like this carry-on at all, so she sometimes pushed me in an old pram until we were well out of town. I remember one day when the farmer had a walk along to the field where we were pulling sugar beet. He had seen the pram and thought there was an infant in it. We told him that we took it to carry home sticks for our fire. He accepted this explanation. Those farms were sometimes three or four miles out of town.

Spring soon came around and Mother was quite well again. It had been a rather lonely winter, as we were about the only travellers staying in the town. The houses which the travellers had lived in for the winter had been pulled down, and council houses were being erected. Father had had to sell the horse, so we were really down that springtime. However, he went away on his own up to Blairgowrie and came back three days later with a lovely yoke which his brother Andy had given him. The pony was young and perfect. We could pay Uncle Andy at any time—when things brightened up.

42

We were eager to get out of the house, so we left it in April.

My spirits soared as we left Brechin behind us. We joined Uncle Andy and Aunt Nancy at a farm near Meikleour. His married sons, their families, and Bella and Willie later joined us with the children. Later we went back up Glen Isla as we had promised to do the turnip-thinning for 'Hearken the Grouse'. Isla was not there and I was a bit disappointed. Daddy pearl-fished the Tay after that while we picked strawberries and raspberries. Then we spent some time just travelling from camp to camp seeing other travellers and having ceilidhs with them. We went half-way up Argyllshire then made our way back again—leisurely and happily.

We were in no hurry to return to the loneliness of the council house, so Daddy found a potato merchant between Alyth and Meigle who was desperately in need of people for the potato harvest. His camping site was nice and cosily sheltered with broom. We noticed a bell tent at the other end of the site. Daddy and the other families who came with us erected winter dwellings, with the fire inside, as October would soon be in. The potato harvest would not be starting for a fortnight.

We awoke the next morning to hear a howling wind, with sleet battering on the canvas, and it persisted during the day. At about one o'clock we heard someone shouting outside. 'Is there anybody in there?'

Father opened the door flap and standing there was a shivering, drookit young man. He spoke with a Glasgow accent, and had in his hand a syrup tin full of water for which he had made a little wire handle. 'I saw the smoke coming out of your lum,' he said, 'and I was wondering if you would boil my can for me. I have been trying for hours to get a fire going but the sticks are too wet.'

'Surely, surely, laddie, come on in,' Daddy told him, taking his wee syrup tin and hanging it on the jocky above the fire. 'Here, this is a great place! You are fine and cosy in here,' the young man went on, edging closer to the fire. 'Laddie dear, you will get your death of cold going about like that,' Mother said. 'Are you biding in the bell tent down there?' 'Aye, missus, we are waiting for the tatties.'

She opened a huge kist and pulled out a vest and shirt and, turning to him, said 'Here, take off those wet things and put these on. Have you no jacket?' 'I'm staunin' in ma wardrobe,' he answered, pulling off his soaking pullover and shirt. 'Would you like a plate of broth?' Mother asked him. 'Would I no' hauf!' he said.

He told us that there were six of them in the bell tent—three from Glasgow, two Fifers and one from Edinburgh. At that time there were droves of young men desperately seeking a livelihood all over the country.

'Oh, that was great, missus! I really enjoyed it. Thanks

135

a lot. I'll away now and give my mates a cup of char.' The young man, as he spoke, was looking for a way out. 'How do you get oot o' here?' 'That wee can will never do for six of you,' Mother told him. 'Have you nothing bigger?' 'It's a' right, missus, we will get a wee sup each.'

It cleared up in the early evening and Daddy built a huge fire outside. Uncle Jimmie was playing his pipes and Daddy was playing quoits with some of the other men.

I was teaching Ricky a new trick. Already he could do some marvellous things. He would immediately dive into the tent and crawl under the straw of a bed, as soon as I or any of us said 'Hornies binging' (police coming) or 'Pooskie binging' (keeper coming). And he would stay there hidden and motionless until he got the all clear. He would go when asked and bring any of us who Mother named. Mother just had to say 'Go and fetch Nancy' (or Lexy or Daddy or any of us) and he would find the right one and tug gently at his or her sleeve. So any of us knew when Mother wanted us. He could also be depended on to guard the tent or a child. One day I saw him being chased by someone's large Alsatian. He ran towards a low caravan and ducked under it. Believe it or not, the Alsatian ran head first into the caravan and stunned itself temporarily. Ricky took advantage of this and hastened to his own quarters. But I must not bore you with tales of Ricky's intelligence.

The young men from the bell tent gradually edged their way down, and stood watching the quoit players. Soon they wanted to have a go and, when Mother waved to Daddy that his supper was ready, he invited the young men to come over with him. Mother had baked some huge scones. (Mother's cooking pots and her girdle for baking were enormous.) Daddy whispered a word in cant which told Mother that the poor boys were hungry. It was so typical of Father, but Mother had anticipated this. She weighed the young men up, without appearing to, then said 'Would any of you laddies care for a bite?' and soon had them all feeling at home.

Soon they were telling us all about themselves. They were absolutely broke and had no possible way of survival except by going at night and stealing potatoes from a field, a turnip or a few eggs from a henhouse. The one from Edinburgh would have died of hunger. He was different from the others—educated, well-mannered and well-spoken but quite hopeless at the art of survival. He lacked the quick wit and shrewd sense of the hard brought-up Fife and Glasgow boys. Mother said that he must have been brought up in plentiful surroundings, with a silver spoon in his mouth. The other boys called him 'the Professor'.

After they had eaten, one of them turned his jacket pocket out, spilling a little heap of cigarette butts on to the ground. Then they all started emptying the shag out of them and rolling it into papers, making roll-ups. 'Where did you get those tabbies?' Daddy asked. 'We picked them up off the road,' they answered. 'Surely to God you are not smoking tabbies off the road?' Mother said. 'You could easily pick up some wild disease doing that. For God's sake, Sandy, give them the price of a packet of Woodbines.' 'Aye, come on, boys, throw they dirty fags into the fire. You will get a packet in the village pub.'

I was much taken with 'the Professor'. He always jumped up to help Mother lift the kettle, or Katie to carry water—in fact, anything that he could to to help. For the next couple of days we didn't have to carry any water nor sticks. The young men did all the heavy work for us. Father and Uncle Andy and Willie and some of our young cousins showed them how to snare rabbits and gave them hares which the dogs had caught, and the women always brought home cigarettes and even sweeties for them. We used to have great fun in the evenings, and this was greatly enriched by the antics and singing, and especially by the comical humour, of these strange boys. To fill in the time Mother and Father were gathering rags and metals, going from door to door with the yoke.

One day they took all six of the boys with them to Alyth. Father gave them a sixpence each and told them to take a street each and go from door to door asking for rags to buy. 'Now, before you go, there is one thing that I am going to tell you. Don't for the peril of your lives touch anything that you see lying about. Country people and village folk often leave their belongings lying outside. It is different here than it is in a big town. But touch nothing. If any of you steal or even lift a safety pin that you see lying, you could make it hot for all of us. You must be honest when you go from door to door.'

Father loosed the pony on Alyth Green. Mother and Katie went in to 'take the town' as they called it. I was to play with the girls on the Green, and look after them. We had left the encampment early in the morning and were to make a day of it.

'The Professor' was back to the Green within an hour, with a large bag of rags on his back. 'The lady wouldn't accept any payment for them,' he said, as he put them on the float. Believe it or not, he collected much more than any of the others. Mother said that the women really liked him because of his good manners and genteel way. They were all very excited because they had received civility from most of the people they had gone to, and were eager to see what was in the bags they had. 'We will have to go to an isolated place first,' Daddy told them.

So, after having tea and something to eat, we found an old road which was no more than a cart track and watched while the boys picked their rags. There were whoops of delight as they found perhaps a perfectly good pair of socks or a shirt or even trousers in the rags. 'Now we have to go to Blairgowrie to sell them,' Father told them. 'There is no rag store in Alyth.' They received about five shillings for their rags, and were as happy as could be. Father only took back the sixpences which he had given them. Few of them had used the money. 'Now, boys,' he told them, 'you can always do that and earn an honest shilling for yourselves.'

Those boys were quick to catch on, and from then on were independent of us. Indeed, they brought home sweets for the bairns and tobacco for Father. On the tattie fields they provided us with much fun and we were really sorry to bid them farewell when it was time for the parting of the ways, and we rather reluctantly went home to Brechin.

43

The new council house was pretty and all that, but we could not do the things that we had been used to doing.

We could not gather rags, nor could Daddy get making his baskets. The old house had had sheds and a wash-house which we could use for this purpose, and no one had ever bothered us. So it was difficult to earn a living. To make things worse, that winter was a very severe one with the earth frozen hard for months, so that we could not get any work on the farms either.

So Katie and I got a job in a mill. (I was now fourteen and free of school.) I can still remember how I hated that mill. Giant machines snarled and lashed out at me with huge iron elbows, and large broad belts screeched and threatened to fly off their wheels and sever my head. Stour and fluff blinded me, and clung to every part of me—even my eyebrows and nostrils. My God, I thought, how could anyone possibly spend all of their working life in such a place? How I pitied those poor dear creatures who did just that. I thought I would rather die.

The work, however, was easy and I escaped into dreams of green fields and noisy little burns, so that the time passed quickly. Poor Katie was not a dreamer, and would sometimes annoy me by bringing me back to the reality of the mill, by saying 'The time goes like a snail in here. It is only eight o'clock yet' or something to that effect. I received twelve shillings and sixpence a week and Katie got a little more than me because she was older. I never spoke to any of the other workers. I wanted no truck with the 'country hantle' and I only spoke when absolutely necessary. I was still smarting from the buffeting I had received at school and avoided any communication with them. It reached the stage where I would scarcely go into a shop. I would take Nancy or Lexy with me and send them in.

We used to play a horn gramophone and make fun dancing and carrying-on in the evenings, but the complaints of neighbours soon put a stop to that. Mother sometimes went out to a few houses, more or less out of loneliness, but

Father was very lonely and frustrated because he couldn't get doing the work that he was accustomed to. He sometimes paced the floor restlessly. To make it worse, very few of our traveller friends visited us. They said that they didn't want to come in-about the new house, and shame us up.

One day Katie wrote to Lady Hardy, who had been wondering why Daddy's baskets had stopped coming. She visited us a few days after that, in spite of the severe weather. She was a tall lady, very simply dressed in a mackintosh and brogues, but breeding exuded from her. She talked to Daddy about his problem and even accepted tea from us. 'But willows are not dirty, Sandy. I don't see why they should stop you making baskets.' Daddy explained to her that willows had to be boiled in winter, and told her of the fussiness and antagonism of our neighbours.

For them it was just too much that they should have to live beside tinkers, and the least thing sent them running with complaints to the Council. One day Mother had carried in a bag of old clothes which she had received from a lady. Next day a man from the Town Council had come down and told Mother that they had had complaints. He inspected every room of the house, saying 'You cannot turn it into a rag store.' Father and Mother explained all this to Lady Hardy.

'Goodness me,' she said. 'Your house is like a little palace. I know of lots of houses where they think that the bath is for holding their coals—with children running about verminous and dirty, and the ashes almost meeting you at the door. Better they would get on to them instead of pestering you people.' 'Aye, we ken that, Lady Hardy, but those people are not tinkers,' Mother said. 'You know how they feel about tinkers. These people that you are talking about, who cannot even keep their own noses clean, are the worst ones for complaining.'

'Well, I'll tell you what I'll do, Sandy,' Lady Hardy went on. 'I shall arrange for willows which are already peeled, and ready to use, to be sent to you. You just tell me the length and type that you want and the quantity. They are not expensive, and you will have to pay for them yourself after you get going, but the first lot you shall have free. All the prices and varieties will be enclosed with the first lot. Then you can send for them yourself—always allowing four to five days for them to get here. Now I shall have a word with the housing factor, and see that you are not stopped from making your baskets.'

About a week later the willows or 'wans', as we called them, arrived. Bunches of different lengths and thickness, and one bunch which had been buffed to a beautiful tan colour. Daddy was as pleased as if some one had given him a hundred pounds, and my fingers were itching to get weaving those lovely wans. I sat up so late that night, making a flower basket, that the mill bummer was booming away before I awakened in the morning.

It went for a full ten minutes, sending its doleful sound all through the town, letting the mill workers know that it was ten minutes to six Time to come along and get started to work. We worked from six until nine, when we were released to go home for some breakfast. We started again at ten and worked until dinner time, one o'clock. Then back at two until half-past five, and all our comings and goings were accompanied by the noise of the bummer. However, the machines and I were on a bit more friendly terms now. They did not threaten me so much and I had even come to like them a bit, admiring their ingenuity.

I read a lot in the evenings at that time—anything that I could lay my hands on. From a veterinary book I learned about tetanus, rabies, anthrax and many more animal diseases. Then from somewhere I acquired a huge illustrated volume of Darwin's theory. I marvelled at the man's cleverness and imagination, but was not one bit convinced by it. I also read and re-read the Bible, trying to understand it, but many parts of it were as unacceptable to me as they were to Mother. However, I did—even at that early age— believe that there is a Master Craftsman, 'God' if you like, who would and could be near to us and guide us in our journey through life, if we asked Him to.

The baskets which Daddy made with the cultivated willows were much neater and easier to make, and he was happy again. This made Mother happy too and, of course, all the rest of us as well. The council house was a bit like prison to us, and that is the name that we gave it. There were so many restrictions.

Poor Ricky was not supposed to be there at all. *No dogs* was one of the rules set down and he was perhaps the unhappiest one amongst us, having to be cooped up all day. Twice it was reported to the Town Council that we had a dog. I used to pop him into the washing boiler when the men came to the door, covering him with clothes and putting the lid on—after warning him to be quiet. He seemed to understand and remained there soundless until I came and gave him the all clear. We lied like troopers to the housing man. Mother opened every cupboard and lifted the bed covers to let them see that no dog was in the house. I used to stand there with my stomach crined into a knot lest Ricky should come out or start barking. He was only a dog after all! The neighbours knew that we had a dog but couldn't prove it. Another restriction of 'the prison' was our inability to play the pipes and have a bit of fun in the evenings. Even singing could be heard through the thin walls as plainly as if the singing was in the same room.

How we missed the old houses with their tumbledown sheds, wash-houses and thick walls! In spite of the fleas and inconveniences I am sure all of us would have jumped at the chance to go back to one of those old houses, but they were being demolished. How we all longed for the return of spring!

On Sundays we all used to walk for miles to where some friends were living out. We were almost tempted to give up the house and join them, but they were being so harassed by policemen moving them around that Daddy decided against it. Had he had sons he would not have hesitated, but it was too much for one man with only women and girls. Friends offered the help of the strong arms of their young sons, but Daddy declined. He did not want to be dependent on anyone.

This was one of the reasons why travellers preferred to have male children. While they loved all children, they were very proud to have lots of sons. The girls were given as much as, if not more than, the boys—but when grown up they had to serve and obey their brothers. They were brought up to consider it their duty to serve the menfolk, to wait on them hand and foot in fact. I can remember one day watching a girl washing a huge heap of shirts and socks, belonging to her brothers and father, and I actually envied her—wishing that I had brothers to wash for and to serve.

April came at last. The two girls had their two hundred attendances at school and we were impatient to get out of the town. (At that time attendances were taken in the morning and in the afternoon, each full day counting as two attendances.) We were allowed to leave the house as long as we kept sending back the rent.

However, it was to be late in May before we did get away. Nancy, Lexy, and I took the measles. (Katie had had them as a child.) I was really ill with them. The rash just wouldn't come out. Mother had tried for three days to bring it out, and in the end gave me a little sulphur mixed into jam. That must have done the trick, because soon I was covered with it. Father and Mother nursed us day and night.

'I wonder if it's worth while gan up to "Hearken the Grouse",' Father said, on the day that we left the house. 'His tatties will all be planted.' 'We could still get the neep-thinning,' Mother answered. 'He will not be very pleased if we don't go back after promising.'

So it was back up Glen Isla again. The first week out we were like cattle that had been let out to pasture after being cooped up in a reed all winter!

44

Our first stop was only a few miles from Brechin where a few of our friends were staying: the Boat Camp, it was called, being near the South Esk river.

The men were pearl-fishing the river. I soon found my way there too, and walked along the path on the bank. I wondered, as I walked, why there nearly always was a path along river banks. No matter how isolated the river was, one could always find a path along the bank. Rounding a bend on the river, I suddenly stopped and stared. It was so beautiful. Masses of forget-me-nots bordered the river, almost into the water. May flowers carpeted the banks and fragile-looking wood anemones, which would rather die than live anywhere but under their beloved trees, grew in profusion in the wooded area. Many other species of wild flowers were also to be seen, and their mingled scents were so pleasing. I filled my eyes with the beauty around me, and breathed deeply the wonderful scents. Oh this is so good, I thought, after the stour and noise of the mill.

I found a green patch and lay down on my belly on the cool green grass. It was a very warm day and numerous sounds of nature filled my ears. The husky, yet somehow high-pitched, whispering whistle of a mouse told me that it had a nest of young down there somewhere near. The sound of grasshoppers, jumping-jacks we called them, and the gentle rustle of a nearby shaking ash tree. What secret of nature made the leaves of this tree rustle, when every other tree was still and quiet? Was it the gossip of the woods, whispering about its friends and neighbours? The river, too, seemed to whisper and mumble as it glided past. I lay there in a state of ecstasy. With the beauty, the scents and the sounds of my surroundings, Nature had completely enchanted me.

So I was more than annoyed when I felt the ground moving under me. 'God pity you, you silly wee black moudie!' I said aloud. I knew that there was a mole down there, and I thought that if he could burrow through the hard ground, then he could easily burrow through my soft body. Not that I had ever heard of any such thing, but I was not going to lippen on it.

So I got up rather hastily and found that it was several minutes before my eyes would focus properly and before the earth would stop spinning under my feet. So deeply had my emotions been spellbound with so much beauty.

45

I started to walk back along the river bank and as I approached the old road where we were camped I heard little voices cronying. Pushing through the bushes, I was surprised to see Lexy and Nancy.

'What are you two doing here, so close to the river?' I shouted as I neared them. 'Who let you away down here?' They ran towards me, and I could see that they were both considerably distressed. Suppressed tears escaped when they saw me and both of them clung to me.

'What's the matter?' I asked. 'Is anything wrong?' 'The two of them are making murder,' Nancy said. 'We are looking for you.' 'What are they making murder about?' I asked, knowing that they meant Daddy and Mammie. 'Where is Katie?'

'They are making murder about pluffen,' Nancy answered, 'and Katie is away somewhere.' 'Oh, shaness!' I said—quickly feeling the pocket of my pinafore, where an ounce of tobacco lay. I had put it there for safety, and had forgotten about it.

'Come on, Chookie, on my back. Biff, you run in front of us.' (I had nicknamed Lexy 'Biff' because she always seemed to run biff into you, instead of stopping, when she came near.) We ran until we were some yards from the tent, which was in an opening surrounded by blooming broom bushes and scattered trees. I put Chookie down and told the two of them to be quiet.

Then we moved silently through the broom bushes until we were near the tent. The wee girls were inclined to giggle, but I whispered to them to be quiet and we keeked through the bushes at Mother and Father.

Making murder they certainly were—that is, if it is possible to murder cups, plates, pots and pans. At that very moment a large defiant iron pot was having its head banged against a stone by Mother. Broken dishes were scattered all around. Daddy was sitting on the bank, shouting 'Go on, Maggie! You're doing fine, girl! That's the way to do it! That's the stuff to give them!'

He had his chanter in his hand and, putting it to his mouth, started playing *Maggie Mac-a-Dougall*. 'I'll make chanter and a' into atoms if you don't shut up!' Mother shouted, running towards him and trying to snatch the chanter. 'Aye, would ye?' Father said. 'Come, come, hussie, or I'll put a knot on your brow.'

I took the tobacco out of my pocket and removed the paper from it. It was black bogy roll and I pulled it out its full length and threw it near to where they were, without them noticing. It lay there shining like a black serpent. Father spotted it first after some minutes. 'Look Maggie, what has come up through the ground to you! Look what the Devil has sent up to you! There, at your heel, woman!'

Mother turned and, seeing the tobacco, turned again and ran at Father. 'You had it all the time!' she was shouting. 'You dirty round-headed beetle! Breed of the beetles and meals!' and she went on shouting nicknames at him. Father grabbed her two wrists. 'May I be as low as my dear mother, Maggie, if I had that tobacco.'

Mother knew that he would not swear an oath on his dead mother for all the tobacco in the world. So she turned away from him and, walking over, picked the tobacco up. 'Devil-sent or Heaven-sent, it's going into my pipe,' she said.

Suddenly she stopped in her tracks. 'The weans! Where's my weans?' she shouted. Father jumped up, saying 'My God! They are mebbe away down to the water!' They were about to take off when I shouted to them, and came forward out of the bushes.

'So it was you that went away with the tobacco!' Mother said. 'I forgot,' I answered.

I started to sweep up the broken dishes with a brush which I made with broom, while Father and Mother sat puffing away at the mischief-making weed—both of them giving little bursts of laughter every now and then, thinking about the silly way that they had been carrying on. Soon I had all the debris in a heap. 'I will dig a hole and bury that,' Daddy said.

Just like that Katie came in-about. Her brows came down when she saw what was left of the dishes. 'What are folk supposed to mak' meat in, or eat out of?' she said. ('Folk' in this case being herself and the rest of us. She had a habit of calling herself 'folk'. 'Folk cannae get doing this,' or 'Folk cannae get peace,' and so on, always saying 'folk' instead of 'I'.)

Soon Father and Mother were friends again, and the only problem was how we were going to get food made. 'We are going to do well for a cup of tea,' Father said, 'and I could do fine with a fine big bowl of reeking, yellow tea.'

Katie and I slipped away anonst from our parents, and cut across fields to where there was a farm and cottar houses. 'Who is going to ask for the dishes?' Katie asked. 'We will both go,' I said. 'I'll try the farm and you try the cottars.' I lied to the farmer's wife, saying that the box which contained all our pots and dishes had fallen off the cart somewhere without us noticing.

Then I looked closely at the woman and knew that her soul was tormented. 'I am sorry, lady,' I said, 'I can see that you have troubles enough without me troubling you.' 'Nae trouble lass, nae trouble.' I could see that she controlled herself with great difficulty as she spoke. Her hands were like a fledgling's wings and her eyes showed that she was fighting desperately to hold on to her reason. She was fumbling about in the kitchen, dropping dishes and pacing about.

'You seem a bit upset, lady. Have you had an illness in the house or perhaps lost a loved one?' 'Weel, I lost my father, but he wasnae exactly a loved one. What do you think the auld bugger done, after me keeping house and looking after him this ten years since my mother died? He has left the farm and near a'thing tae my brother. My brother married the maid and Father has made me be just a lodger in my ain hame. This maidie is mistress of the farm now, and I am nothing.'

'Have you nowhere else to go?' I asked her. 'A sister or other relative, perhaps?' 'I have nae sisters,' she answered. 'He expected me to go and bide in the lodge at the end o' the road. And right enough he left me a few hundred to keep me, but hell and buggery! The farm should have been mine!' She ranted on in this way, stamping about and working herself up to a very high pitch with the power of her own thoughts. 'The dirty unthankful auld sod. I hope the worms are enjoying his flesh.'

I felt *my* flesh creep at those words, and I stotted backwards down the three steps at her door. Then I ran, round the steading and down the farm road, to the cottars where Katie was standing talking to the cottar women. I was shaking and I knew that all the blood in my body was down at my feet. I had darted through a herd of cattle being taken out to a field without realising properly what I was doing.

'Gosh, lassie, you look like death. What's wrang? Are you feared o' the coos?' the cottar woman asked laughingly. I looked at her and nodded a lie, thinking to myself 'Feared of coos indeed! No, missus! I'd be less feared of a nest of vipers than of some of the people that I meet!' Katie whispered a cant word asking what had happened. 'Horn moich mort,' I answered in cant, meaning 'a pure mad woman'.

One of the cottar women went into her house and returned within minutes with two cups of hot tea and a piece of bread and jam for each of us. 'Here, tak' this, it will help you. The coos widnae touch you. I'm surprised at you being feared of them.'

We left the cottar houses with a large iron kettle, a pot and two or three stone jam jars which would serve as cups until we got some.

Now we had to go back past the farmhouse. I told Katie about the woman as we walked along. 'God bless us, that's terrible,' she said. 'She must be completely mad!' (Of course we spoke a lot more in cant than I write down. I don't want to irritate you with it.)

We just rounded the corner of the steading, when who did we see there but the woman from the farm. 'What's echt ye?' she asked. 'Why did you run away? I have a pile of dishes here for you. Come round and get them.' 'Oh, I'm sorry,' I told her. 'My sister was shouting for me to come. She was feared of the coos,' I added mischievously. I was beginning to come to myself again.

We followed the woman round to the door of the

farmhouse and, sure enough, she did have a pile of really beautiful dishes. Flower-bedecked plates and cups, and two pots. 'But these are much too good to give away,' I said. 'Och, tae hell! You are as well to get them as that bitch of a wife that my brother has.' Katie and I exchanged looks.

'We would rather not...,' Katie began. 'Aye, ye will! Here,' she said, putting the dishes into a bag and thrusting them into Katie's hands, 'you are the biggest.' We hurried away, and once out of earshot I said to Katie 'What did I tell you?'

Katie was a bit frightened now. 'She will mebbe say that we stole the dishes,' she said. 'I would not like to be using the dishes anyway. Not for the Pope o' Rome. We will go down the burnside and dump them somewhere.' We did this, throwing one here and there into the thick undergrowth so that they were completely hidden. Then we scoured the old pot, which the cottar woman had given us, with sand from the river bed.

You might think that we threw away the dishes lest we should be accused of stealing them. This was not the reason at all. We were afraid to use them. Afraid because of the spiteful way that she had given us them. Spite against her sister-in-law, I mean. Afraid that the evil in the woman would somehow be transmitted to the dishes, and from the dishes to us. So we wanted no part of them. This may sound like madness to you, but it was our way of thinking.

Once or twice on the way home I shuddered when I thought of the woman's words about her dead father. 'I hope the worms are enjoying his flesh.' What a horribly evil thing to say!

Traveller people revere the dead—and especially their dead parents. If you ever chance to be talking to a traveller, during the conversation, he or she will almost certainly say 'My father once told me', 'My mother used to say', 'My mother liked this or that', 'That was my father's song' or 'My father's part of the country.' Even very old people do this.

So our parents never really die but go on living in the hearts of their children—and what the parents had been, the children mostly become. Wayward sons and daughters suffer great remorse on the death of a parent and nearly always will change their ways, and be as their parents would have had them. A bit late perhaps, but not too late for their own children and their other parent.

People often ask me about religion, and if we travellers have any special religion.

Well, some travellers—who have been living in towns for a generation or so—have taken up a special religion, but before that we didn't have any specific religion. However, we did have a very strong belief in God and feared him. Our whole code was always to put others before ourselves. Even strangers. We believed that if we were selfish with anything, then we would have no luck with it. I have seen parents, when food was very scarce, trying to make their children take what there was—in vain. Even very small children would say 'I'm not hungry, Mammie. You take it.' All the family would refuse to eat until the food was shared equally. It was considered a very selfish thing for any member of a family to eat anything past another. Women would walk all day looking for food, but not one morsel would pass their lips, unless they knew that there was food at home for the rest of the family.

Travellers also believed that if they did wrong they would be punished for it. They would often say 'No better could happen to me, after what I did.' Or, 'I should have shared my tobacco with Johnnie. Now I have lost it. That's what I deserve.' No matter what evil befell them, they thought that it was a punishment for something that they had done. I too am sure that it happens this way. Doing good is rewarded by God sending good luck to us and all evil is punished by bad luck. It is a simple code which really works.

Evil-doers often seem to thrive, but there is no rest for them. No matter how much they deny it, their conscience eats their heart away and they do suffer. A clear conscience is the greatest thing in the world to have. As Daddy often had told me, 'You have no need to fear God, man , nor the Devil if you do no evil.' Evil, in our minds, was deliberately hurting or causing another human being to suffer. The worst evil was to be selfish. This was usually stamped out in childhood. Each member of a family, even after marriage, was expected to share any good fortune with his parents, sisters and brothers. Even if one of the family was a real waster, the others would never see him or her in need and not help.

Don't think that I am trying to make out that travellers were angels. Far from it. They cursed and swore a lot, drank a lot of spirits and fought among themselves. They had many other sins—but at the same time they were full of love for each other. Illness or bereavement was deeply felt and even travellers who were complete strangers would give their last penny to help anyone ill or bereaved. Collections were nearly always taken for a funeral. Travellers never for one moment forget that it could be their child or their parent, sister or brother who is suffering or dead. Apart from that, the real hearfelt feeling is there, and this more than anything helps to sustain those who have lost a loved one.

I have wandered again. So I'd better get back to the Boat Camp.

Katie and I were eagerly and scornfully telling Mother and Father about the wicked farm woman. 'There must be twelve or more rooms in that farmhouse, Mammie, yet there is not enough room for only three of them,' I went on. 'Her father left her hundreds of pounds and a lovely cottage, but that is not enough for her—and her with neither husband, bairn nor birth. Oh, Mammie, they are all mad, those country hantle!' 'Haven't I told you a thousand times, lassie, that they are nearly all mad? They think that they are never going to die. What in the name of God would one lonely woman want with a big farm?'

This was the travellers' way of thinking.

46

Next day we were on the road again, and stopped at Eassie. where there were about six other travelling families. Most of them were working at farms in the district.

There was all the usual talking and dealing between the

men, while the women talked of other things and gave or exchanged articles of jewellery. Travellers love gold rings, earrings and brooches but mostly they gave them away after having them only for a short while. They had had the pleasure of owning and wearing this beautiful thing or things. Then they would give them to someone else, so that they too could have that pleasure.

'Hearken the Grouse' was delighted to see us when we finally arrived up Glen Isla. We had been joined by several other families of relations. 'It's about time you were here. The neeps are growing like bracken. They will be no easy job now. What kept you, man?' he asked Father.

Mother sent me up to the farm for milk. Meeshie came twittering to the door, and behind her a beautiful young lady. It was Isla, but a very much changed Isla. So poised. So ladylike. I was a bit overawed by the change in her, and could only stare. 'Bessie, how you have grown!' she said. 'Aye, like a tattie on a stick,' I answered her, eyeing her beautifully curved figure. 'Oh, you will soon fill out,' she said.

'Hoppity died,' Meeshie informed me. 'Kate, Jean, Jess! Come and see who's here!' she shouted. Little Cameron was first to rush out. Then his mother and the other two girls. They plied me with home-made cakes and scones.

Our stay up the glen was very pleasant. No worries about food. Work by day and fun, games, dancing and singing in the evenings. We sang as we worked too: keeping time with the movement of the hoes. Often we played a game as we worked. Someone would make up a verse of a song to a well-known tune, then the next one would add a verse, and the next one—and so on. Often they were about people we knew or about each other. Sometimes they were very funny and there was much laughter. The little children played about at the foot of the field, making mud pies.

Ricky was always amongst them. He often caught young rabbits but would not kill them. He wanted to play with them. Most of the others had greyhounds and kept them tied up most of the time. The men often went hare-hunting with their greyhounds. Cameron gave them permission to hunt all over his land, and he loved to accompany them. He had acquired two greyhounds—just for the fun of having them to compete with the travellers' dogs—and Cameron's extremes of emotions, when watching the dogs, provided the men with many a laugh. We could hear his voice booming down the glen, even when they were quite a distance away.

Traveller men loved a hare chase, and they would give a quite unreasonably high price for a good dog. The dogs were patiently trained, and they had to be biddable—stopping, even when nearly on the hare, if their masters wheeped to them. They were also trained to run silently, as more often than not they hunted anonst to farmers, and silence was essential.

Ricky had complete freedom up the glen. He no longer chased the fowls. He was also very biddable. Cameron's shepherd would often take him with him when he was attending to the sheep.

One morning, very early, we were awakened by a stick coming 'walt' off the canvas of our tent, and an unknown voice shouting 'Get up oot o' that, and see what that damned dog o' yours has done!'

Mother always was a bit crabbit in the mornings and the rude awakening made her even more so. 'God bless me, man—whoever you are—you must be haunted. The Devil himsel' must be haunting you or else you would still be sleeping. It's only five o'clock in the morning. What dog are you speaking about? We have no dog but a wee canny collie, that would run a mile wi' the fright o' a midge.' 'It's that wee canny collie that I'm looking for. Come oot here and see what the wee bugger has done!'

Daddy had been getting into his trousers and was first outside, with me almost at his heels and still barefoot, and we instantly recognised a shepherd from further up the glen. We had seen him once or twice. 'What has the doggie been doing, shepherd?' Daddy asked him in a respectful voice. 'Open your een, man, and you will see that he has stolen twelve of my sheep,' he answered. 'Where is the wee bugger?'

I looked around and, sure enough, a number of sheep were scattered around grazing within the enclosure where our tents were. (Cameron had fenced off a sizeable piece of land for us.) 'The dairy lad seen that doggie wi' the sheep.'

There was no sign of Ricky, but I guessed he was somewhere within earshot. So I started to sing. 'Jewgell plank yer nagens, Jewgell plank yer nagens,' to the tune of *One, Two, Three A-leerie*. This meant 'Doggie, hide yourself.' The shepherd gave me a queer look, and Daddy said to him 'Dinnae heed that lassie, she is no' just all right.' 'Poor soul,' the shepherd said, 'ye would never ken tae look at her.'

'Noo dinnae get me wrang,' he continued. 'My sheep had gotten oot on the road and your wee collie must have rounded them up and took them doon here and put them in beside your tents.' 'I'm really sorry, shepherd...,' Daddy began. 'Sorry? Weel, dinnae be sorry, just get the wee rascal till I hae a bit look at him. I have seen him once or twice with Cameron's collies, but I never paid much attention to him.'

'One of Cameron's dogs is his mother,' Daddy told him. 'Aye, and if I'm not misteen, one of my dogs is his father,' the shepherd answered. 'I'm needing a young doggie to train, so get a haud of him for me. If he's a' as good, I'll give you a good price for him.' 'I dinnae think the bairns would part with him,' Daddy told the shepherd. 'We have had him since he was a puppy. I'll tell you what, come back doon some night when I have had a chance to speak to them aboot the doggie. They just might give him to you.'

'Aye, and when I do come doon there will be nothing here but the marks of your tents. I ken you mist folk of auld. You come and go like the mist on the hills.' Many people called us 'the mist folk' because of our (to them) mysterious comings and goings. 'I promise you,' Daddy assured him, 'we will be more than a week here yet.'

The rest of the camp was just beginning to stir when the shepherd rather reluctantly rounded up his sheep and departed. When he was out of earshot, I shouted at Daddy. 'Ye ken fine, Daddy, that I wouldn't part with Ricky for a hundred pounds. How did you tell him to come back? Wheeple on Ricky for me.' Ricky came in-about, hunkering, when Daddy whistled. He had hidden under the hedge near the gate.

I had lit the fire and made tea whilst the shepherd was

talking to Daddy. I handed him a bowl of tea saying 'Daddy, do you hear what I am saying to you?' 'Aye,' he answered. 'Now come and sit down here till you hear what *I* am going to say to *you*.' He was sitting on a tattie hamper near the fire and I sat down on my knees near him. 'Now listen, Bessie, Ricky doesn't have much of life when we are in the house all winter. He never sees daylight hardly. Ye ken yoursel' how you have to wait for darkness or hide him in the cart before he can get out awhile. You are being selfish, Bessie. Think on the fun Ricky could have here, working among the sheep. Plenty of freedom and plenty to eat and drink. Furthermore he would be doing what he was born to do. If you love Ricky you will give him to the shepherd. I'll get you another dog.'

'Oh, Daddy, please dinnae ask me to part with Ricky! Ye ken yersel' that I could search a lifetime and still never find a dog like him. He knows every word that I say, Daddy. He can even feel my every mood. I just cannae part with him.' 'Weel, weel, but I think you're being very selfish. That's not like you, Bessie. Think about it.'

I was very moody for the next three or four days, neither singing nor talking while we worked. I walked about with Ricky in the evenings. I wanted no human company. I mostly made for the banks of the Isla. The murmur and whisper of rivers had always been soothing to me and had somehow seemed to give me a clearer vision of things. I sat down on a tree which had fallen across the river.

Ricky sat beside me, looking up at me and whimpering a little. I spoke to him as if he was a human. 'It's all right, Ricky, I won't fall in the water. You must understand, Ricky, that it is because I love you so much that I am giving you to the shepherd. You really will be happier here romping through the glen.'

Just then I heard someone approaching. 'Plank, Ricky!' I said, as I shinned up a tree. I soon saw that it was Cameron who was coming. We had been taught to hide ourselves if we heard or saw strangers, especially if there was no one with us, as one never knew who could be prowling about.

Somehow I was really pleased to see Cameron. I

dropped down from the tree and, calling on Ricky, ran to meet him. Cameron had his knapsack on his back and I knew that he had probably walked about twenty miles looking for Charlie. He had these days when he seemed to be away with the fairies, but only in this one respect. He truly believed that Prince Charles was hiding from the redcoats in the glen.

He seemed pleased to see me too. 'Who is with you?' he asked. 'What are you doing here by yourself?' 'Well, you have been away by yourself looking for the Prince and I'm here by myself looking for something too. Cameron, if you had to go and live in a town would you take your dogs with you? You see, the shepherd in the next farm up the glen wants Ricky to train as a sheepdog and Daddy says that Ricky would be happier there.'

I was so unprepared for the gulder of a roar that came out of Cameron's mouth that I nearly slithered down the bank into the water. 'The dirty sleekit weasel! So he wants Ricky, does he? Well, he will bloody *want* him! Geordie, my shepherd, told him that Ricky was a natural-born sheepdog, and I mysel' wouldn't ask him back from you. Devil take the sleekit bastard! I am sorry, Bessie, for cursing. Geordie's heart and eye are in that wee collie and if you think that the cratur would be happier in the glen, then Geordie is the one to give him to.'

Cameron ranted on all the way to the encampment. I was very tired as I had to run all the way to keep up with his giant strides. He was too riled to notice.

'Man, Sandy, I am disappointed in you, man,' he greeted Father. 'Would you be giving Ricky to that damned foxy shepherd? I tell you, man, that if the doggie stays up the glen it will be with *my* shepherd and Bessie can stay with me where she can see him every day. I'll see that she wants for nothing. What do you say, man?' 'You had better ask her yourself,' Daddy answered him. He could see that Cameron was in a precarious frame of mind and didn't want to upset him in any way.

Of course I didn't stay on with Cameron—but Ricky did, and the other shepherd would find, just as he had predicted, that we had disappeared like the mist. None of us wanted to get mixed up in any differences between him and Cameron.

So we just slipped away.

47

We parted company in Alyth. Most of our relations wanted to find a place where they could stay until the raspberries started. Daddy wanted to pearl-fish the Tay so we held out through Blairgowrie and Meikleour looking for a camp, but all the old camping sites had notices up saying *No camping*.

We were all tired and hungry so Daddy pulled into Meikleour Green. 'Bessie, go and see if any of the houses will boil a kettle of water for you. I am gasping for a drink of tea. Katie, loose the pony and let it graze for a while. Maggie, here, take this half-crown and see if you can get something for the weans to eat.'

I picked up Mother's big milk can, put two dozen clothes pegs which Daddy had made into a little basket and, with the basket on my arm and the can in my hand, I started back along the village.

I scanned the houses as I went, looking for the most likely ones. Houses which were very spick and span, without a weed in their lawn or garden, were seldom occupied by people who would waste their time boiling water for a tinker. Houses with curtains drawn almost to meet were usually occupied by rather reserved timid people, some of whom were afraid of tinkers. So I chose a house which was homely-looking. Not really untidy, but with odds and ends lying about outside. Some old flower pots, a child's battered barrow, a dog's dish and two kittens were near the door.

However, the lady who opened the door to me was very suspicious-eyed and a spinster, I was sure. 'What do you want?' she asked. 'Could you please oblige me with some boiling water?' I said. 'Indeed I will not,' she replied. 'You should think shame of yourself. Coming here begging. A young girl like you. You should be away working.' 'I am not begging, Missus, I will give you some clothes pegs for the water.' 'I have no need of your clothes pegs nor baskets either. I have plenty of everything. Now get going before I set the dog on you.'

I felt my anger rising, and could not refrain from saying 'You are indeed a very lucky woman, having plenty of everything. Yet you can't even spare a little boiling water. No wonder you could never get a man.' Her facial expressions were impossible to describe, but I didn't wait to look at them. I was down the drive and over the dyke before she could let the dog out—dodging a short-handled sweeping brush which she hurled after me.

A few doors further along a young woman kindly boiled her kettle for me. 'There is tea in the can,' I told her. 'I just need the water, as there is nowhere around here where we would be allowed to make a fire.' 'What about milk?' she said. 'Only if you have enough and to spare,' I told her. While waiting for the kettle to boil, I asked her about the woman who had chased me. 'Oh, that's Mrs McDiarmid. She has her aunt living with her just now.' 'I think it must have been the aunt that I saw,' I told her. 'Oh aye, it would be. Mrs McDiarmid and the bairns are away to Perth today.'

I counted out a dozen pegs and laid them on the doorstep. 'Hoots, lassie, I'm no' takin' your clothes pegs. Na, na, water doesn't cost much.' 'Please tak' them,' I said. 'It is more than good of you to boil the water for me. They will be lucky to you.' 'I am needing pegs but I have nae money. I do have some strawberry jam left from last season, and I have a guid coat that would fit you. I have gotten ower fat for it.' So we came to an agreement, thanked each other, and I hurried back to the common lest the tea would get cold.

As I approached I could see the village policeman talking to Daddy. 'Oh, oh,' I thought. Then I noticed that both he and Daddy were laughing heartily, so I came in-about. The policeman and Daddy were joking with Lexy and Nancy. There were old stocks on the village green and they were telling the girls how people who didn't behave were put into those stocks and battered with rotten eggs and such. Those old stocks might still be there, but it is many a year now since I was at Meikleour.

'Well, I'll awa' and let you get your tea,' the policeman said. 'Ye ken I have to do my job.' 'Surely, surely,' Daddy answered him. 'I just stopped to rest the pony and get a cup of tea. I had no intention of camping here.'

As we took the tea, and bread spread thick with butter and strawberry jam, I told them about the woman who had thrown a brush at me. Mother and the girls laughed, but Daddy said 'And who told you that the woman couldn't get a man?' 'Nobody told me, I just ken,' I answered him. 'Ye ken too much, wee woman. Far too much for your own good. I thought I had got it through your thick skull that this temper of yours was to be curbed. Could you not just have walked away and said nothing? I never want to see or hear of you losing your temper again.'

'Aye, you are good at telling me not to get angry, but what about yourself? What about Wallace the policeman, back on Coupar Angus Green, eh?' I shouted this. Mother butted in here. 'What's this about Wallace the policeman?'

I suddenly realised that I had let the cat out of the bag and I gave Daddy a look which said 'Very sorry'. He gave one of his deep sighs and told Mother all about it. 'I didn't tell you because I didn't want you putting the bootchlach on him,' he told her. 'Bessie, he nearly killed your cousin Hendry. I had good reason to get angry.' Katie too shouted at me. 'You are awful clever, aren't you?' 'Dinnae you two start,' Mother said. 'Come on, we must haud on the road and see if we can get some place to stay.'

After walking four more miles we were confronted with an iron gate with barbed wire along the top of it. This barred the entrance to the old road that we had been going to. A large *No camping* notice had also been put up. 'God pity them,' Mother said. 'They would deprive us of daylight if they possibly could.' It was about eight at night by this time, and we were all a bit weary. 'I will have to back-track to some of the farmers that I know,' Father answered.

So we turned back, and just as we came down past the Beech Hedges we saw an old man pulling a barrow. 'That's awful like my Uncle Hughie,' Daddy said. Sure enough, it was Father's uncle. Father ran to meet him and greet him.

'In God's name, Uncle, what are you doing on the road at this time of night?' It was about half past nine by now. 'Where is Belle your wife?' 'She is getting a drop of tea made in a house back there,' the old man answered.

'On the road at this time of night? Weel ye may ask, laddie. By the look o' things, we'll have to put our tent up on the road. We came all the road from Dunkeld yesterday and we had to lie out in a wood all night. Then, do you know the quarry this side of Spittalfield?' When Father nodded, the old man continued. 'Weel, we got there about four o'clock the day, and pitched our tent—but we never got time to tak' tea, meat nor water. A young whelp of a policeman came and tore the tent down about us and ordered us away. This is becoming a hard world to live in, when a body cannae even get the breadth of himself to lie down in.'

Katie ran to meet old Belle when we saw her coming along the road with her basket on her arm and a wee can, with the tea in it, in her hand. 'Oh, Sandy and Maggie! I am bonny glad to meet you,' she said. 'I don't know what this world is coming to,' she continued. 'God bless me, but folk are getting worse every day that you rise. I had to give that woman back there the last threepenny bit that I had about me, for this wee can of tea.' 'Well, never mind, Uncle, sit doon and tak' your tea.'

Then Father told them of our fruitless search for a camp. (Nancy and Lexy were sleeping on the cart. Mother had made a sort of bed for them.) They wouldn't take their tea without sharing it—even though we lied and said that we were not long after tea. There we were, sitting at the roadside at the foot of the beech hedges. Mother and Father and the old couple talking, Katie looking after the pony which was eating the grass off the verge of the road.

I had been in a cantankerous mood all day and now I was beginning to let self-pity creep in. I really missed my dog. What was he doing now? I thought. Was he missing me? He was so timid. Would the shepherd's other two collies take advantage of this? So my thoughts wandered on and on until the tears came. 'Ricky, Ricky,' I kept repeating silently.

160

Mother's quick sensitivity soon felt my despair. So she turned and called me up to where they were sitting. I had been sitting a bit apart. 'Bessie, come here a minute. Come and get a wee draw of this pipe. I'll bet you never seen a pipe like that before,' she said as I came near. I was glad that darkness had fallen to hide my tears. 'Look, it is a real meerschaum. Old Hughie will not be pleased until I take it.' It was indeed a lovely pipe. I could feel the elaborate carvings on its head and the curve of the shank. 'Take a draw. Are you cold or hungry?' 'No, Ma,' I answered. I really wasn't. My heart was too full for Ricky to feel anything else.

'Come, we had better get off the main road,' Daddy said. The time had flown so swiftly that darkness had fallen on them almost unnoticed, so engrossed had they been in their crack. Katie and I pulled the old couple's barrow. Daddy put both of them into the cart, and led the horse by the head. He knew almost every inch of the countryside and soon we stopped at an opening to a moor. We had travelled about two miles up an old road first. Daddy hated to disturb the sleeping girls, but it was necessary. He tethered the pony after unyoking it. Then he threw a tent cover over the trams of the cart and another over the cart itself. Mother then made a bed under the trams for the girls and one for Hughie and Belle under the cart. Katie and Daddy and Mother and I took a blanket each and cooried down around about the outside of the cart.

Old Belle was a natural comedian and, instead of falling asleep, we must have talked and laughed for at least another hour. She seemed to think our situation highly amusing, and even I laughed in spite of myself.

The root of a broom bush digging into my ribs awoke me quite early in the morning. The sky was rosy-golden, way in the east, as it reflected the sun's magnificence. I got up quietly and looked around me. We were on a broom-covered moor riddled with rabbit holes. I wandered across the moor but could hear no sound of water. Then I wandered around the edge, where the moor was palinged in, knowing that there must be a watering place for the cows and sheep in the fields around the moor. Soon I found a trough and by pressing down the ball in it I could get clean water. I ran back and very quietly got our big black tea can out of the cart and a cup. I also took a bucket which we kept for the pony. It always hung from the side of the cart when we travelled.

Coming back, with the can and bucket full, I drew my breath in through my mouth with delight as I caught sight of some white and black baby rabbits amongst the ordinary ones. I put the can and bucket down and ran and caught a beautiful little black one. I carried it back and sat down with it on my lap. 'Don't tremble, wee cratur. I would never, never hurt you. Who are you anyway? An enchanted princess maybe, or are you a prince?'

I was just turning it over to see, when I felt a presence near me. It was a man and he was quite near. Quite a young man, wearing country tweeds, but having the unmistakable air and bearing of our Scottish gentry. He lifted his deerstalker hat and said a polite 'Good morning'. I had not moved from the spot where I sat, but I was ready to bolt if needs be. 'Good morning, sir,' I said.

48

Somehow the gentry seemed to be the only people who had any understanding of us travellers. In their own way they had many of our own characteristics. Their love of privacy to do what they really wanted to do. Their acute awareness of another human's inner feelings. Their love of freedom to wander at will. Their ability to give without meddling and interfering with our lives.

They often owned large estates, and large stretches of water, and often Father had obtained a permit to pearl-fish on their waters. They didn't say 'Don't take my salmon. Don't frighten the wild birds or take their eggs.' This was the unspoken agreement which all intelligent travellers respected. Trout we would take—from the wee burns where there were no salmon. The gentry were also tolerant of weaknesses and ignorance.

But to get back to the one standing no more than five yards from me. 'Where are your people?' he was asking, having recognised me for what I was. 'They are not far away,' I answered him. 'What is your name? he asked. 'Reid, McLaren, MacDonald?' His natural instinct told him that I would bolt if he came any nearer. I did not answer but looked up into his grey-blue eyes. They showed a mixture of emotions—humour, compassion and understanding.

'We will be out of here within the hour,' I told him. 'Don't be frightened, child. I am going to take off my haversack, take out this paper—see—and this,' holding up what I took to be a pencil. 'Now just sit as you are for a few minutes, please. I am going to draw you.' In no more than five minutes he had done just that. Then he turned it round and held it up to let me see it, and there I was—complete with rabbit, black can and bucket, long straggly hair, bare legs and wrinkled cotton dress.

'Oh, that's clever!' I really was excited and started to go towards him for a better look, then stopped suddenly and backed away again. He smiled and said 'Would you hurt that rabbit? I would no more hurt you. I will come with you to your people.' 'No, no! Please sir. They will die of fright. We had rather a bad day yesterday.' 'Alright, here is a penny for you. Here, catch!' He flicked a coin towards me and I caught it between my hands.

'Is this your ground?' I called to him, after he had restored the bag on his back. 'No, it isn't,' he answered. The little rabbit still sat happily on my knee. It hadn't bothered to run away and seemed quite content where it was. The man started to walk away without another word. 'Goodbye, and thank you sir!' I called after him. 'Bye-bye!' he called, lifting the deerstalker.

At first I thought that he had given me a penny but, looking again, I recognised it to be a sovereign. I waited until he was out of sight, said goodbye to the rabbit, picked up the water then, on turning round, I saw my father coming towards me. He had probably been hiding in a clump of broom, and watching, while I was talking to the man. 'Daddy, look! A gold sovereign!' 'Oh shaness! He must have made a mistake. He must have thought it was a ha'penny. Did he say who he was?' 'No, Daddy, and I never asked him.' 'Give it to me and I will see if I can catch him. You go back with the water.'

Daddy took the sovereign and hurried away after the man. The rest of them were all up. Old Hughie was sitting wiping the drones of his pipes. He had taken them to bed with him the night before. He adored his pipes and never let them out of his sight.

'Did you see your father?' Mother greeted me. 'Aye,' I answered—and then told her where he had gone. 'Silly man. He should have kept it,' she answered. We had been for more water, washed ourselves and had our tea before Daddy did return.

'He wouldn't take the sovereign back again. Poor soul, he nearly lost his life with some foreign trouble that he got abroad. He is so pleased to be well again. He told me that when he was lying there, as weak as water, in hospital he came to his senses.

'"I was always a go-getter," he said. "Like an endeavouring ant, never satisfied no matter how much I acquired—and very intolerant of the very poor, especially you tinkers. I also discovered that my own friends like myself were too busy to visit me in hospital. Yet poor cottar people and other tenants on my father's estate would sometimes walk for miles to the door of the hospital, not daring to ask to see me but sending in fruit, eggs and other things which they could ill afford. At first I was annoyed with them. How dare those common people make themselves so familiar with me! Then I realised that they really cared, which was more than I could say of my so-called friends. As I lay there I asked myself to what purpose has all my endeavouring been? What was I chasing? My friends, too, what was their haste that they could not pause for more than a few minutes to comfort me? My outlook has changed. When I think of how close I was to death, life is so precious. In future I will make time to enjoy it. Nearly all my friends and relations think that my illness has made me a bit queer in the head, and are waiting for me to join the gang again, but they will have a long wait. So you keep that sovereign and spend it as you will. You can even get drunk on it if you like. Just enjoy it."

'I thanked him,' Daddy continued, 'and left him sitting drawing a cow in a field.'

49

Daddy had two big bowls of tea before we took to the road. Katie and I took turns of pulling the old folks' barrow. They had no family. Their two sons had been rather cruelly taken from them when they were just infants of six months and two and a half years. Whether it was the shock of this cruel deed, I don't know, but they never had any more children.

'Tell me about your babies, Granny,' I asked her, as we sat having a rest at the side of the road. 'Oh, it's a lang, lang time ago now, lassie. It was the simplest way done that ever you did see. I was barely nineteen at the time. Coming through Blair Atholl I seen a wee tattie-beetle hanging at the door of a shop, and I took a notion to this wee tattie-beetle. So I went and I gave sixpence for it. Then I went to the back door of the inn and got my milk-can full of porter for another sixpence. Hughie was waiting for me at the end of the town. I had wee Jimmie on my back and the young wean in my oxter. All was going fine. We sat and drank the porter and had a smoke. My hand to God, sister! That is all the drink that we had. Then I lifted the wee tattie-beetle out of my basket, saying "Look what I bought."

'Well, that done it. His face changed colours, and he come a slap off my face. "You dirty off-taking mare," he said. Did I ken, sister, that he would be so angry because his nickname was Beetle? He came another slap off me. "Hell to my soul if I'm going to let you off with that!" I told him. Then I took the wean out of my oxter and unbuckled the other one off my back. I laid the two weans down at the side of the road, wrapped in my plaid, and I made a breenge at him. Soon skin and hair and oaths and curses were flying.

'Then the hornies came and lifted us and put us in the jail. They took my weans away and I never seen them again. They likely put them into one of they Homes and, them being so young, they could soon forget us. Well, I was demented. I sat at the door of the police station, roaring for my weans, but all I got was thrown into the jail again. This went on for months. I'm telling you, sister, that I lost my weans ower the heid of a tattie-beetle. I swore then that while grass grows or water runs I would never go back to Blair Atholl and I never did.'

My heart went out to her, as I could imagine the profound suffering which the loss of her children had caused.

Many other travellers had had their children taken from them. Well-meaning, but blind and stupid; authorities pounced on encampments and forcibly took our children on the least pretext. Those children were healthy and happy, and deeply cherished, even though they might be running about barefoot and covered in mud. We lived on the earth, slept on it, ate off it, and often became the colour of it as we grew older. The earth to us was not dirt. How could it be dirt? Everyone, everywhere, kings and queens as well, depended on the earth for almost everything that they ate. If the earth is dirty, then everyone must have dirty insides. It will not harm anyone's outside either. So the children would never have come to any harm although they were sitting making mud-pies and almost covered with it.

The Homes that these children were put into couldn't hold them for long if the children were about six or older. They would await their chance and escape at the first opportunity. They would approach the first travellers that they met and they would be hidden and looked after, and soon returned to their parents. Then the parents would have one hell of a time hiding from, and dodging, the authorities.

Often too the authorities, the so-called 'welfare people', would almost force the parents of young girls to put them into service. The places that they put them into were often hotels or big houses with very miserable owners. The girls were slaved, and almost starved, in most of these places. The welfare workers were blindly unaware of this, and often said 'Those tinkers are very unthankful and lazy' when the girls ran away back to their people.

Some girls did stick it out and eventually made quite good marriages with some man who was not a tinker, but they were very rare.

I do not mean to imply that all hotel-keepers, or people with big houses to keep up, were the way I have mentioned, but there were some like that—and those were the ones who agreed through 'the welfare' to take tinker girls. Probably because they could get no-one else to stay with them and slave for them.

50

I don't know how far we had walked the quiet roads when I looked ahead and saw, coming towards us, on an old cycle, a boyish figure with long red hair glinting in the sun.

I immediately dropped the old folks' barrow and ran forward. Surely it must be my cousin Jessie! No-one, nowhere, had that particular colour of hair. We fell into each other's arms, rolling on the grass verge, after she had thrown down the cycle. Then we ran back to my folks. After cuddles and kisses all around, Daddy asked her where they were staying. 'Uncle Willie is with us, Maggie,' she informed Mother. 'That is a wonder,' Mother said. 'He never comes down this way.' 'They are all working at the hay on a farm not far from here,' Jessie went on. 'Are you coming to stay beside us?' 'Will we get leave?' Daddy asked her. 'Uncle Sandy, he is the nicest farmer I have ever met.'

Soon we came to the camping ground: a strip of woodland about five hundred yards from the farm. Mother was pleased to see her two brothers with most of their children around them, some now married with places of their own.

'There is surely going to be a blue moon,' Father greeted Mother's brothers. 'I never thought to see you in this part of the country, Willie.' 'Well, man, only one thing took me down here and I suppose you can guess what it was.' Uncle Willie was Hendry's father, the Hendry who had been beaten up by Wallace the policeman at Coupar Angus.

'Dinnae tell me that you came down here to get at the policeman,' Daddy said. 'Did you think I was going to let him off with it?' Willie said. Then he started laughing. 'Wait, Sandy,' and to Mother, 'Wait, sister, till I tell you about it. All this time I've been swearing revenge and saying, and thinking about, what I was going to do to him, and when I did get the chance I couldn't touch him.'

'I made Jess (his wife) put my clothes on. My bonnet, boots, everything. As you ken yourself, she can work at the hay as good as any man. So she went out to work in my place and I slipped away into Coupar Angus. I ploutered about Coupar Angus all day playing my pipes and letting on that I was blind peevie. Then I went out to the end of the town and lay down at the side of the road. Sure enough, I did not have long to wait for the bold boy coming. I was lying watching him with the tail of my eye. I heard him putting down his bike, and saw him come towards me, but I just lay still muttering like a drunk would. Then when he was almost on me I grabbed his legs and got him down, and jumped on top of him. But Sandy, brother, he started to greet like a wean. I just hadn't the heart to hit him, but I near shook the insides out of him. Then I pulled the trousers off him. Boots, bonnet and drawers too I tore off him. I never seen a man so feared. He couldn't lift a hand to save himself. I never left him with one stitch on. Then I made off through the wood and I pushed all his clothes away down deep into a rabbit hole, and cut across the country and home!'

Uncle Willie was a big strong brute of a man and I could well imagine the policeman's fear.

By this time someone had the tea ready and soon we were all enjoying it with scones which one of the girls had made. Jess was anxious to tell us the rest of the story. So Uncle Willie let her have her say.

'The Perth police were here questioning us,' she said. 'None of our men have been away from the camp since we came here, we told them. They never let on what they were doing, or who they were looking for, but the next day the farmer and the grieve told us that they had been asking if all the men were working, and if any of them had been off on such and such a day. Both the farmer and the grieve assured them that all six men had worked until eight that night.

You see, Maggie, they never paid close attention, or they would have kent it wasn't Willie, and I sort of kept a bit away from the grieve when he came to the field!'

The farmer had no objection to us staying, and I was very happy to be with Jessie. Daddy and Mother and Lexy and Nancy went away to the river all day, taking the yoke. Katie and I stayed at the camp and we enjoyed ourselves very much in the company of our cousins. Soon, however, our money ran out—the sovereign as well—and, as Daddy had not been lucky at the pearl-fishing, we had to try and earn something. But Daddy was never happier than when he pearl-fished. He knew almost every inch of the pearl rivers in Angus, Perthshire and Argyllshire. It gave him a sort of mystic contentment which affected us all, so that we were all very happy.

'Bessie, do you remember how to make wire baskets?' 'Of course I do, Daddy.' 'Weel, you ken that I like to have your mother and the weans with me at the water. So I'll get a hank of wire and you can make a few tomorrow, but watch the folks' weans when you are using the sothering iron. Katie will help you to fill the baskets.'

So when they came home from the river the following evening, Katie and I had ten wire baskets, filled with moss and peaty earth, and the prettiest ferns we could find. Katie had exchanged one with the farmer's wife for eggs, oatmeal and milk. A cottar woman gave her a sizeable piece of sootie pork and some potatoes for another one. So we had quite a nice supper ready for our folks coming home from the river.

Old Belle and Hughie wandered here and there nearly all day. He, playing his pipes to anyone who would listen, and her, telling fortunes—mostly to servant girls in farms. They brought home an ounce of tobacco for Father and Mother.

So all was very serene and peaceful.

51

One day who should come in-about just when we were at our supper but Hendry Reid. 'Well min,' Father greeted him, 'and what wild wind blew you in this direction?' 'I heard you were staying here, Sandy, I just wanted to see my auld friens.' Hendry could be very charming when he liked. 'Sit down and Maggie will give you something to eat,' Father told him.

Then an old tramp-man came wandering in off the road and asked if he could boil his wee can at our fire. 'Surely, surely, auld yin. Sit down and rest and it won't take a minute.'

Daddy got up as he spoke and gave the old man the most comfortable place there was to sit on, an old upturned dup tin. 'Wait,' Katie said and she placed an old coat on top of the dup tin for the old man to sit on. I went to fill the wee can with water, Daddy to refuel the fire. Mother was at the door of the tent feeding the ravenous girls.

So none of us was paying attention to what Hendry Reid was doing—until we heard the old tramp-man give a howl of pain. He was holding his mouth and he, and dup tin as well, had fallen backwards. Hendry Reid was laughing as if to burst.

'What happened?' Daddy asked, as he helped the poor old man to get up. The poor soul was unable to answer. He just kept holding his mouth. Then Mother noticed a big spoon lying on the ground half full of skirlie, so she quickly brought a cup of milk and told the old man to sip it and hold it in his mouth.

'I want to ken how this happened!' Daddy's face was white with anger. Lexy said 'It was Hendry Reid, Daddy. He asked the old man if he liked skirlie. The old man said yes, then Hendry handed him the spoon of scalding skirlie, and the old man burned his mouth with it.' Now skirlie is peculiar in that it does not steam like most other foods, no matter how scalding hot is is.

Father turned to Hendry, saying 'You done that deliberately, didn't you?' Then Father grabbed him by the throat and held him backwards over and very near the fire. 'We'll see how you like being burned! I've a good mind to roast you and feed you to the crows. I would be doing the world a good turn.'

Father's own feet were almost in the fire. The girls and other children started screaming and the noise brought Uncles Willie and Hendry and their boys running up. Uncle Willie pushed both Daddy and Hendry Reid away from the fire, and they both fell to the ground, but safely, away from the fire. Uncle Willie then bodily lifted Hendry saying 'Leave him to me, Sandy. I don't know what he has done but it must have been bad to make you get so angry.' He then gave Hendry two or three hard kicks on the behind, saying 'Run, Danny! You are a disgrace to all the breed of you!' (Danny was the Reids' nickname.) 'Run! And never come within a mile of us again or I will mak' you into hawk's meat!'

Mother and Katie were trying to make the old man comfortable. The cool milk was soothing to his scalded tongue and throat. The old tramp's mouth was not as bad as we had supposed.

He was a beautiful old man with a pure white beard and surprisingly thick white hair. His eyes were the colour of ripe blaeberries. His hands with very, very, long tapering fingers explained his being on the road. Tramps are in no way like travellers, except for their wandering on the roads. Whereas travellers loved to be in company, tramps were almost always alone. They had none of the cant language. Many of them had come from good families, but were too highly sensitive to criticism and rebuffs. Those long tapering fingers might have created wonderful things—had not some coarse, insensitive, fellow human-being been over-critical. There just happen to be such people. They cannot help being that way, and they suffer profoundly from their over-sensitive nerves.

'You will know me if we ever meet again, miss!' he said to me. 'Oh, I am sorry, sir,' I answered, 'but you are still very much worth looking at. I wish you were still my age, then you and I could get married!' I was hoping that he had a sense of humour, as I sat down on my knees in front of

171

him. The sore blistered lips did manage a wee smile. So I relaxed. 'That must be sore,' I said. 'I will see if I can find anything to ease the pain.' 'Your mother is going to make something for it,' he told me, 'but I could do with another cool drink. My tongue is burning.' When Mother saw me run to give him cold water, she shouted to me to give him milk instead. 'The milk will help heal it,' she said. 'Give him it all. We can do without milk.'

She had gathered a pile of chickweed and was packing it into a clean syrup tin. She had bored holes in the tin and had put a wire handle on it. She then poured some olive oil on top of the chickweed. Then she broke a small twig off a tree and peeled it, using it to pound and stir the boiling oil and chickweed. I didn't stay to watch what she did after that, but went back to the old tramp.

'Were you ever married?' I asked him. He shook his head and said, '*She* married my brother.' 'Is that why you took to the road?' I asked him. 'Now, missie, what possible interest could all the tales of my life have for you?'

Just then Jessie came bumping along on her bike, her red hair flying behind her. 'I got some, Auntie Maggie!' she shouted, holding up a paper bag. Inside the bag there was a honeycomb. 'You would never believe how far I have biked. Here is your shilling back, Auntie. She wouldn't take any money for it.' We sat talking to the old man, until Mother came over. The chickweed and olive oil had somehow changed into a green salve. 'Now, auld yin, we'll have you as good as new before you can say Jack Robinson. Keep the honey inside your mouth and spread the ointment thick on your lips,' she told him.

Meanwhile Daddy had erected a wee tent, just a tiny wee one. 'You lassies mak' a bed for the old man.' I filled a pillow case with straw, crushing and thumping it to make it more comfortable, while Jessie made the bed. 'Dinnae be feared,' Daddy told him. 'No one on this ground would harm a hair of your head.'

None of them had mentioned Hendry Reid since. They didn't want to put themselves off their sleep by getting all het up about him. 'You weans be quiet and let the old man sleep. Come and I'll tell you a story.' Soon all the weans were gathered round Mother listening to her tales of fairies and witches. By this time the men had all been fed, and the children. Now the women would have theirs, wash the dishes, tidy up, then get together for a crack. Katie was doing Mother's chores.

I was so wilful that they just left me alone. It was more bother than enough, trying to force me. In the right mood and with no distractions I could whisk through all the work, but if I showed no willingness to start it, Katie just went and did it.

The old tramp stayed a few days. We all tended to him as best we could, or knew how to.

Before he left he took a small leather bag out of his jacket pocket. He opened that bag and took out another cloth bag. Inside this there was another. So he went on until finally the long thin fingers pulled out a gold lever watch. The chain was made of beautiful black human hair, and the key for winding it had a large jewel at the top of it. 'My father's watch,' he said. Then, fingering the chain, 'my mother's hair. I want you to have it, Sandy, I will soon have no use for it.' 'No, praise be to God, I will not take your watch. Put it back where it belongs. Don't worry about us, old man, we will surely get enough for our needs.'

Daddy helped the fumbling old fingers to replace the watch and the old man shuffled away.

52

The next day was a Sunday. Daddy never pearl-fished on Sundays. We usually walked miles that day visiting other travellers or had other travellers coming to us. This particular Sunday we had visitors—two men, two women and about six weans. Cousins, nieces, nephews and others.

During the conversation one of the women said 'What did you do with the wee collie you had, Sandy? Did you lose it? It came to us at Meigle last week. We gave it food, but it chewed through the rope that I had tied it with and was gone in the morning. Davie Higgins said that it came to them too. It is going round all the camping places looking for you.'

'Are you sure it was Ricky?' I asked her. 'Aye, I am sure. Would I no' ken the same wee dog?' 'He must have run away from the shepherd,' Mother said.

I would give Father no peace until Ricky was found. Daddy's poor legs were sore with cycling from camp to camp. My intense delight at having Ricky back was reward enough for Father, but I knew that he could not have rested anyway until he did find him. I took Ricky and cuddled him and apologised a hundred times to him.

Daddy's luck changed and he found some beautiful pearls. Katie and I had managed to get enough food for our needs by trading the wire baskets.

Many of the folks just gave us out of the goodness of their hearts as, being in the country, they could have made them for themselves. There were hundreds of travellers who would never have survived but for the generous goodness of the warm-hearted Scottish people. Hay and corn for the horses, and milk, flour, oatmeal and even eggs were given by many farmhouse folk. Bakers in the towns, too, played a big part in our survival: all the bread, cakes and scones which were left over at night were put into paper bags the next morning and we could have them for no more than a penny a bag. Butchers, too, played their part—and grocers. All this was in the time of the Depression. People were like that in those days and right up until the time the Welfare State came into being.

This Welfare State—which was meant to help people—brought much suffering, confusion and unhappiness to many travellers. The middle-aged and older ones, especially, were forced to go and live into houses all the time and were given money for doing nothing, like wild birds in cages. They didn't want this at all. They didn't want to pace the floor of a house all day doing nothing, and there was no way that they could carry on with their own ways of making a living while living in a council house. Many were given jobs, but this too was hell for most of them. They hated being tied, and having no freedom—nothing but the same monotonous routine every day. It was not laziness. Most travellers are good workers. It was the compulsion that irked them.

The women, too, had a very difficult time. Being quite unused to making a wage spin out for a week they just couldn't do it. Before, they had lived from day to day. Some were good days, some bad days, but every day had had to look for itself. Now they had to compete with the often very critical women of the 'country hantle'. They would overdo themselves cleaning their houses and keeping their children as clean and as tidy and as quiet and well-behaved, as the 'country hantle' were.

The effort was too much for them. They would nag and plead with their husbands. 'Take me out of here. I will be dead before I know that I have ever been living. Am I going to waste my life polishing and cleaning inside a rockery of stones? Never seeing my friends, nor a soul belonging to me?'

There was much discord and misery. So often they would take off and go and search the country for a place to camp or put a caravan. Then perhaps some other welfare people would take over and the whole thing would start all over again.

This is still going on to this day.

53

Now back to the farm—where we all got work at the harvest after the hay was in. Then Daddy took us all for a wonderful tour of the Highlands after he sold his pearls. We enjoyed the company of many friends in our travels, returning to Brechin in late autumn.

That winter is very hazy in my memory. Perhaps because I have no wish to remember it.

Daddy talked much with us and especially with me. Mostly words of wisdom about the rights and wrongs of life. 'Bessie, remember my words.' We were planting the garden together that late autumn—strawberry plants, Michaelmas daisies, spring cabbage and other things. I remember him saying 'I will not be here when the strawberries are ready.'

He died early in May but had not been bedded, although he had been complaining. I ran out of the house screaming 'Oh, my Daddy! My Daddy! My Daddy!'

Friends took us off to live with them in Blairgowrie. Daddy was buried in Caputh cemetery where many of his forebears lay. When we returned to our house in Brechin about two weeks later, every personal thing of Daddy's had been taken away and burned—except his pipes. This is the custom with travellers.

I was still in a very dazed condition. I had not stopped shaking. I went out and somehow found myself on the banks of the river Esk. There I lay down on my belly, sobbing and crying, and talking to Daddy. 'Daddy, I am sorry for all the times I was wilful, thrawn and wicked. I am sorry for telling you lies. Please forgive me, Daddy! Oh God! How am I going to live without my Daddy?' I tried to picture him and remember things about him. Strangely, it was all memories of his laughter and his jokes that came. Oh God, what am I going to do? My thoughts kept racing. What am I going to do? How am I going to bear life without him?

Then it suddenly came to me that these were selfish thoughts. Had Daddy not told me never to be selfish? Then is grief no more than a form of selfishness? I am thinking of myself. How will *I* make out? How can *I* bear this? Of course this is selfish.

So ran my thoughts as I lay there crying. Then I realised that the shaking of my body had stopped and somehow I felt calmer. I sat up and looked around me. I felt as if I had just come back from some far-away place.

I stood up and for the first time saw my surroundings. I had seen nothing on my way down here. Nor indeed since Daddy died. Now I noticed a wild blossom tree, all the different shades of green around, the budding willows. I fingered a bush which Daddy had planted, forget-me-nots and May flowers. How beautiful, surely the most beautiful of all our wild flowers, is the May flower. I bent and didn't touch, but rather caressed, their soft petals. They felt vibrant and so alive somehow. I had always loved them, and so had Daddy.

'I'll take a bunch of you home to Mother,' I said.

During the picking I heaved two or three deep sighs like Daddy used to, but I was calm as I made my way home.

Calm and ready to take up life again.

It is doubtful whether the cant, the language of travelling people, is really a language at all—consisting as it does of many words from other languages.

The cant was very useful to travelling people—but only to them. One word could have many meanings and could carry the meaning of a whole sentence, depending on the situation and the tone of voice. In fact, a traveller could appear to be having a normal conversation with a non-traveller—but in reality be giving a message, perhaps a warning, to any traveller listening.

It could be used very cunningly indeed. In wartime it was possible for any intelligent traveller to write home what appeared (even to the best censor) an ordinary simple letter. But it could contain much information to a traveller, such as where the sender was and what was going on around him.

This cunning way of using the cant is dying out rapidly and there is no possible way of retaining it. It is quite impossible to teach to anyone: only by being brought up with it from infancy can it be properly learned. We can *tell* the words to anyone, but *how* to use them is something which will be lost once the travellers of this generation are gone. Even now only about 150 to 200 words remain.

Only a few words are used by young people and children—and those few are almost as familiar to non-travellers. For now that children are integrated in schools, and young people work side by side with non-travellers, some cant words have been integrated too. But most of our young people are so pleased at being accepted, integrated, that they refuse to learn much cant—and even angrily rebuke their parents for using it.

As you will understand, this is a constant source of frustration, disappointment and sadness to the older folk. They see their children and grandchildren—brought up in towns and almost the same as non-travellers—look blankly and stupidly when cant is spoken, not understanding what is being said.

And so, sadly, the cant—like the traveller people themselves—is now almost extinct.

a' all
> *a'thegither* altogether
> *a'thing* everything

abee 'Leave him abee' means 'Leave him alone'

aboot about

agley in the wrong direction

ain own

Anee! an exclamation of sorrow, pity

anonst unknown (to somebody)

ashet a large plate

auld old
> *auld yin* old one

avree away

awa' away

bairn a child

bang a crowd, a number of people;
especially domineering, overpowering people

bannock a thick round oatmeal cake

barricade the central and taller part of a winter camp (tent) off which the sleeping quarters were built. The fireplace was in the middle and a hole in the roof of the barricade allowed the smoke out

Barry! a cant word to express pleasure

beak to warm – in the sense of warming uncomfortably, as on a really warm day

beal to fester

ben inside

besom a sweeping brush; an unpleasant woman

biddable obedient, cooperative

bide to stay, reside

big, bigg to build

blaeberry a bilberry

blaggard a blackguard, a bully who is cruel for fun

blether to talk nonsense

bogy roll a coil or twist of tobacco

bootchlach a curse (the word obviously comes from the Gaelic word buidealaich with the same meaning)

bothy a stone-built hut used as living quarters for unmarried farm labourers

brae a hill

breenge a lunge, an attack

brose   a kind of porridge made of uncooked oatmeal, boiling water, and salted

buck   a person who has taken to the travelling life or who has only one parent of traveller stock

buckie   a small seashell, particularly a winkle

bull tree   an elderberry tree

bullyrag   to order someone about, to demand a lot

bummer   a factory siren

Burker   an intruder (The word originated from William Burke who, in the early nineteenth century, murdered people to provide corpses for medical research or teaching. Travellers were often a target for his activities.)

burn   a stream

bursary   a scholarship

butt end   the broad end ('To go to the butt of the heart' means to go against the grain, hence 'Work goes to his butt' means that a man does not like work at all.)

by   'you by anybody' means 'anybody but you'

caber   a large heavy pole used for tossing at Highland Games; a slang word for a man's penis

cam   a whitening material for stone floors

camp   a traveller's tent

cannae   cannot

canny   a word used by travellers, meaning
    1 sensible and safe   2 carefully moving around, as well as cautious
    cannyways   cautiously

carlin heather   bell heather

ceilidh   an informal evening gathering for conversation, singing and music-making

chanter   (in a bagpipe) the pipe with finger-holes on which the melody is played (There is also a separate pipe similar to this used for practice.)

chitties   tripod irons with a chain and *cleek* to hold a cooking pot over a fire

chuckie stane   a small smooth pebble

cleek   a large hook

coo   cow

coorie   to crouch or snuggle down

cottar   a farmworker who lives in a tied or rented cottage

couldnae   couldn't

country hantle   the settled house-dwelling country people

coup   to fall, tumble, overturn

crabbit   cross, peevish

crack   sociable conversation; to chat, gossip

cratur   creature

crine   to shrink or shrivel

crony   to talk confidentially and quietly to a close friend or crony

crook   an iron hook and chain on which a kettle or pot is hung over a fire

Cruelty 'A Cruelty' was how we referred to an Inspector of the Royal Society for the Prevention of Cruelty to Children – or to any official of a Local Authority

cuddy   a donkey
    cuddy-back   piggy-back

cutty   short
    cutty semmit   a short underskirt or undershirt

da   daddy

dae   to do

dander   a stroll or a short walk ('To go for a dander' may also mean to stroll away to relieve oneself.)

dee   die

didnae   didn't

dinger   'to go one's dinger' is to be extremely angry or worried about something, to make a great fuss

dinnae   don't

docken   the dock plant

doddle   to dawdle

doon   down

dottle   the half-burnt tobacco remaining in a pipe; the dregs of anything

dram   a large measure (of whisky)

drone   one of the three single-note pipes of a bagpipe, of which the bass drone is the longest

drookit   drenched, soaked

dropping   giving birth

drumly   applied to stream water, this means disturbed, muddy, unsettled; so applied to a person it means he or she is confused, has uncertain thoughts, is 'mixed up'

dup tin   a large tin (usually a tin which had contained sheep dip)

dyke   a stone wall

echt   'What's echt ye?' means 'What's troubling, worrying you?'

een   eyes

eechie nor oichie   nothing at all, not a sound ('He never said eechie nor oichie' means he never said one thing nor the other.)

ettling   being eager or impatient to do something

ewe-necked   used to describe a horse with a weakness in its neck and which trots with its head held to one side

fae   from

fash   to trouble, to worry

friens   blood relations

fu'   full, tipsy

gaen   going

gailie   a *barricade*, the central and taller part of a winter tent (described under *barricade*)

gan (gang)   to go, to travel
    gan-aboot   travelling about
    gan-aboot person   a traveller

gansh   to talk too much, to bore someone by talking in too great detail *gant*   to yawn or gape, to gasp for something

garron   a strong horse you could depend on, even though it might be of an inferior breed

gee   a fit of ill temper (Hence 'to tak' the gee' means to go into a sulk.)

gey   very

girdle   a griddle, a heavy iron platter used for baking

git   a tiny wee bit

glaggen   the sheen over a field of grain or hay or over a moor

gloaming   dusk, twilight

goot-bird   a bird which imitates the call of other birds

greet   to cry or weep

   gret   cried, wept

grieve   a farm manager or foreman

guid   good

guddle   to catch a fish with the hands

gulder   a loud angry shout

gurly   applied to water, the sea or the weather this means cloudy, rough, so applied to a person it means he or she is grumpy, in a bad mood

hae   to have

hame   home

haneyin' sin   a really wicked, cruel, unforgiveable sin

hap   to dress a child, to tuck up in bed

haud   to hold

hauf   half

havenae   haven't

heed   to pay attention to someone or something

heid   head

het   hot

   het up   to be heated, angry

henny-skinned   goose-pimpled

hippen   a baby's napkin or diaper

hooch   a dance; the shout given during the dancing of a reel

hornies   the police

hoshens   soft coverings for horses' hooves to deaden the noise

hotching   swarming, heaving

huke   a sickle

hunkering   crouching, stooping; sitting on one's hunkers or haunches

hussy   a brazen woman

in-aboot   in-about: a traveller expression which cannot be translated by 'come in' because you do not come *in* to an encampment as you come in to a house. You come within the general area of tents, fire, parked carts and tethered ponies. You come in-aboot from any direction and may move about greeting people at their various occupations in different parts of the encampment.

isnae   isn't

jocky   a fire-iron with a point at one end and a crook at the other on which a kettle or pot can be hung (The cant word is 'snottum'.)

just like that   at that exact moment, suddenly

keek   to peep

ken   to know

kist   a box or chest for storage

knickit   made pregnant

knowe   a small hill

lang   long

larek   larch

lass, lassie   a girl or young woman

lippen   to depend on, to rely on

live out   to live in the open (in tents, as opposed to living in a house)

loup   to jump, to leap

louse   to loosen

> *lousin'*   'loosening' by cutting the twine which bound sheaves before feeding into a threshing mill

lum   chimney

> *lum hat*   a top hat

mair   more

mak'   make

martin hut   a small stack made from sheaves of flax

mavis   a song thrush

mebbe   maybe

midden   a rubbish heap, dung heap; a term of abuse (particularly to a woman)

min   man

mony   many

misteen   mistaken

moudie   a mole

mouser   a moustache

mysel'   myself

na, nae   no, not

nane   none

neep   a turnip

newsing   exchanging news of recent events or about mutual friends and acquaintances

nip   a small measure (of whisky)

no'   not

o'   of

oot   out

orra   odd, unusual

> *orra-looking*   queer-looking, unkempt

ower   over

oxter   an armpit; to lead by the arm

paggering   a beating

peekit, peekish   sickly-looking

peesie   a peewit or lapwing

peevie   drunk, intoxicated

piet   to pitch up sheaves of hay or straw when building a stack

Plank!   a cant word meaning 'Hide!'

plouter   to potter about on trifling tasks in one's own time

pluffen   a cant word for tobacco

poke   a small bag, a paper bag

polis   the police

prig   to plead

puckle   a little

puddock   a frog

puttin' stone   a heavy iron ball or a round stone used for putting; a large stone which could be used at the fire and which did not crack with the heat

quadded   jailed

reed   a cattle pen

reeking   smoking, steaming

reenge   a pot scourer made by tying heather together

rife   plentiful

rive   to eat ravenously, to tear apart

roup   to sell by auction; an auction

rowan   a mountain ash

sair   sore

scaldie   a lower class of town dweller (The word origanally meant 'bare': bare of feet, money, clothes.)

sconce   to tease, especially in a way which belittles a person

screich   the first light of dawn

scull   a shallow wicker basket

seed   a very small quantity

semmit   an undergarment
   cutty semmit   a short underskirt or undershirt

shan   a cant word meaning 'bad', really objectionable, unsavoury, causing shame.
   shan dilly   a prostitute
   shan gadgie   an immoral man
   shan trouble   veneral disease

Shaness!   a cant exclamation meaning 'bad word', 'bad deed' or 'bad situation', but it can be used in many diffferent ways.

sharger   a weakling child or animal, the runt of a litter

single-end   a one-roomed dwelling house

skirlie   a quick-fried dish made from a basis of oatmeal and dripping

skittery   vile, contaminated

sleekit   sly, cunning

sma'   small

snottum   a cant word for 'jocky', the fire-iron

soo   a stack of hay or straw

sothering-iron   a soldering-iron

souch   a murmur, the sound made by people talking or by the wind

soused   drunk, inebriated

spall   to spald, to tear apart

stardied   to be arrested and put in prison

staun', staund   to stand

stook   a small stack of corn; to build stooks
 stooked   stacked
stoor, stour   a cloud of dust, dust
stot   to stagger, to bounce
stroup   the spout of a kettle or a teapot
stupit   stupid
swither   to be undecided about something
tabby, tabbies   cigarette end(s)
tackety boots   hobnailed boots
tae   to, too
tail   a loose woman
tak'   take
tare   a quarrel or disturbance
 'to have a tare with the tinks' means to visit a traveller encampment
 to pick a quarrel for fun
tattie   a potato
 tattie-beetle   a potato-masher
 to give someone his tatties   to give someone what he deserves
thegither   together
 a'thegither   altogether
thrash   scared
thraw   to argue, to contradict
 thrawn   perverse, stubborn
tig   to dally, to trifle (with someone); the children's game of 'touch'
toby   a policeman
tocher   a dowry
toll   a cant word for *skirlie*, the dish made from oatmeal and dripping
trauchled   overburdened, overworked
trews   trousers, especially of tartan cloth
twa   two
walt, welt   to hit someone or something
wans   'wands', long straight willow stems used in basket-making
want   When we say that a person 'has a want' we mean that he or she
 is otherwise quite normal but has an obsession or distorted view
 about some thing (or things). Such a person is usually very touchy
 about the subject and the ability to recognise such a 'want' helps one
 to humour the person.
wasnae   wasn't
waur   worse
wean   a child
wee   little, small
weel   well
 Weel-awyte!   Certainly!
whammel   to turn upside down
whar, whaur   where, why? for what reason?
what like?   how? of what sort?
what way   why?
wheep, wheeple   to whistle

Wheesht!   Hush! Be quiet!

whin   a gorse bush

whittle   a large heavy knife like those used by butchers

wi'   with

widnae   wouldn't

wrang   wrong

yoke   a pony and cart (that is, the two yoked together); to attach the pony
to the cart

yon   yonder, that one

younker   youngster, child